DISESTABLISHMENT IN IRELAND:

Implications For Catholic Objectives In Higher Education, 1869-1879

S. Macpherson Pemberton

University Press of America™

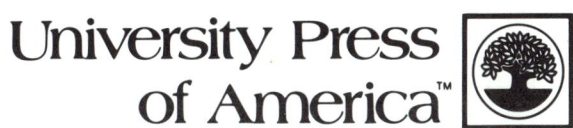

Copyright © 1979 by
University Press of America, Inc.™
4710 Auth Place, S.E., Washington D.C. 20023

All rights reserved
Printed in the United States of America
ISBN: 0-8191-0759-X

Library of Congress Catalog Card Number: 79-64245

Table of Contents

Chapter   Page

　　　　Perface   i
　I.   A Glimpse of the Basic Issues--------------------------   1
　II.   The Church Question-----------------------------------   17
　III. The Land Issue--   41
　IV.   The University Education Problem----------------------   65
　V.   Toward Reform in Higher Education---------------------   87
　VI.   Review and Assessment---------------------------------   107
　　　　Bibliography--   126
　　　　Index---   133

To our parents

Preface

This is a study of the implications of disestablishment for Catholic objectives in higher education in Ireland, 1869-1879. The agitation of the Roman Catholic hierarchy in Ireland for educational equality following the disestablishment of the Irish Anglican Church was really renewed activity. While the Establishment lasted, the outlook for change was always grim for Catholics. On the eve of disestablishment in 1869, they could at least hope for a breakthrough, and a change from the system which they so much detested.

Under the Establishment, Roman Catholics had great difficulty in obtaining university education. It was difficult indeed to get a good education at any level. The higher education system in Ireland consisted of Trinity College or the University of Dublin, the Queen's Colleges and the Queen's University, Maynooth College, the Catholic University, and Magee College in Londonderry for Presbyterians. Such a small number of higher educational institutions were inadequate to meet the needs of the population in general, and of the Catholics who constituted the majority in particular. Up to about the middle of the nineteenth century, there was but one recognized university in all Ireland, the University of Dublin, which contained but one college, Trinity College.

From its inception in 1592, Trinity College was designated as an institution not only for the promotion of learning but also for the cultivation of virtue and religion; and the religion envisaged by its founders was that of the Anglican Established Church. Not until 1793 were Roman Catholics permitted to take degrees in the University of Dublin or Trinity College, and even when that disability was removed, it was nearly eighty years after that before they or Protestant Dissenters could be elected to College Fellowships or Scholarships. In addition, Roman Catholics dreaded the proselytizing influences at the College. Proselytism may take one of two forms: in the original sense, it signifies the attempt to secure, for material considerations, outward conformity to a creed which is not inwardly embraced by the proselyte, or the surrender of children to be brought up in a creed. The latter form of proselytism was held to be immoral under all circumstances by Catholics since it meant cooperating in the bad faith of others. This was surely one area in which the Catholics hoped that disestablishment would bring about a change.

The Catholic hierarchy also looked forward to a change in the mixed system of education. The term mixed education has more than one application. On the one hand, it might mean the mixing of persons of different religious beliefs being educated together, in which case it may be synonymous with neutral education. The Catholics objected to this on the grounds of the consequence of the inevitable mixing of what is taught. It might even imply equal rights in education according to the claims of supporters of the Establishment in Ireland. This latter was quite disillusioning to the Catholics who had seen only inequality in the mixed system. Still further, the Irish Catholics were opposed to the type of mixed education with which the Queen's Colleges were associated, since to them it implied secular education.

In 1845, the three Queen's Colleges at Galway, Cork and Belfast were established by a bill introduced by Sir Robert Peel. Although these colleges were to provide university education for the Catholic people, they soon drew the fiercest denunciations from the Catholic hierarchy, because of the secular nature of the curriculum. The Catholic bishops became even more bitter over their frustrated efforts to obtain a charter for a Catholic university to meet the educational needs of their people. There was Maynooth College, of course, but this had been founded in 1795 for the expressed purpose of training the Catholic clergy. Moreover, Maynooth College, although State supported, was destitute of landed wealth in comparison with Trinity College. It was the hope that there might be some relief from these educational inequities, briefly presented here, that sparked the interest of the hierarchy in disestablishment. But the rising tide of Ultramontanism was bound to produce great conflicts.

Ultramontanism, in general, pertains to the belief that the Pope is the spiritual head of the Church in all countries. In a more specific sense, it is the policy of the party of the Roman Catholic Church that favors increasing and enhancing the authority of the Pope. That was the policy of the Irish Catholic hierarchy under the powerful influence of Cardinal Paul Cullen, Archbishop of Dublin. The hierarchy soon carried over the Ultramontane policy into the educational arena.

But the Ultramontanism of the Catholic hierarchy soon clashed with the Liberalism of the Prime Minister, William Ewart Gladstone and his party. Liberalism devotes modification of political, social or economic institutions for unrestricted human development, as well as government guarantees of individual rights and civil liberties. The greatest expression of liberalism by the Gladstone Ministry was the disestablishment of the Irish Church in 1869.

By disestablishment is meant the dissolving of the connection between Church and State, and the severing of the formal legal ties of the Irish Anglican Church from its sister Church in England. In this way the Liberals hoped to usher in a new era of religious equality and civil justice. This was not going to be easy, however, unless Catholic aims and objectives in higher education were satisfied. Catholic claims for separate denominational education, inconsistent with the Liberals' desires, seemed only to be strengthened by disestablishment.

Disestablishment involved disendowment or the deprivation of the permanent source of income with which the Church was provided. Here is where the question of land comes in, for the Irish Church was rich in lands. Stripping the Church of its wealth, therefore, was really stripping it of its lands. Trinity College as an appendage of the Church was also richly endowed with lands, and was considered one of the principal landlords in Ireland. The land issue, like the Church question, was viewed by the Catholics from the standpoint of the implications it had for the university problem.

The study seeks to provide a closer look at the interrelationship of the questions of Church, land, and university education in Ireland. More specifically, it shows the extent to which the Force of Ultramontanism, as expressed in the Catholic hierarchy's interpretation of disestablishment, complicated the settlement of the university education question. The Catholic hierarchy's insistent demands for educational equity on the basis of its interpretation of the princples of disestablishment, i.e. of justice, equality and freedom, created great difficulty for the British Liberal Party.

The view is taken that the interest of the Catholic hierarchy in disestablishment was in the eventual interest of higher education reform. This fact can be gleaned from the hierarchy's reaction not only to the Irish Church Act of 1869, but also to the Land Act of 1870, the abortive Irish University Bill of 1873, Fawcett's Bill of 1873 abolishing religious tests at Trinity College, and the Irish University Bill of 1879.

Through a grant from the Graduate Division of the University of California, Berkeley, major research for this study was done at the Widener Library, Harvard University. For this I am grateful. To all those who assisted me in the Library of Congress in Washington, D.C. and the New England Depository in Cambridge, Massachusetts, I also wish to express gratitude. Many thanks are also due to Miss. Kathleen Hoffman for willing and efficient secretarial assistance. Finally, I am grateful to my wife, Janette, whose cooperation and support have been a valuable source of encouragement to me.

                                        S. Macpherson Pemberton

January 17, 1979

CHAPTER I

THE BASIC ISSUES

The Liberal Party came into power after Mr. Gladstone received his mandate from Queen Victoria to form a new government on December 1, 1868. At the outset Gladstone declared, "My mission is to pacify Ireland."[1] He thus welcomed the opportunity to lead his first government to do something about Irish dissatisfaction. A year earlier he was moved by the Fenian explosions at Clerkenwell and had proposed an Irish policy along Irish lines. The policy,[2] aimed at attacking the three branches of the Upas Tree of Protestant ascendancy, had a three-fold purpose: religious equality, reform of the land system, and the promotion of equal opportunities in higher education in Ireland.

On assuming power in 1868, the Gladstone Ministry took careful note of the failure of the Disraeli Ministry to find a solution to the age-old Irish problem. Irish affairs constituted the main theme of the first two cabinet meetings of the Disraeli Ministry (March 2 and March 3, 1868), but no consistent Irish policy emerged. During the debate on Irish grievances, the suggestion by Lord Mayo that all churches in Ireland be endowed caused much disagreement on the church question. An ineffective measure aimed at solving the land problem met universal disapproval. Lord Mayo also put forward a plan for a Charter for the Irish Catholic University, but the Disraeli Cabinet insisted that there should be a lay majority on its governing body, and the scheme perished when it was feared that the Irish hierarchy would not accept this.

The role of the Catholic hierarchy is important. It pressed the claims of Catholic Ireland for Improvement in ecclesiastical

---

[1] John Morley, The Life of William Ewart Gladstone (New York: The MacMillian Company, 1911) II, p. 252.

[2] Gladstone used the expression "Upas Tree" figuratively. The tree signified poison and was said to destroy all animal life within a radius of fifteen miles or more.

matters as well as for the betterment of conditions on the whole. The Catholic hierarchy had been agitating in Ireland at least one year before Gladstone announced his Irish policy, and it directed a constitutional movement which soon fitted into the pattern of Gladstonian liberalism. Moreover, the Catholic movement was a powerful factor in the sectional alliances which were formed in the early 1860's and which joined forces with the Liberal Party under Gladstone in 1868. It is true that it was not pressure from the Catholic hierarchy which brought about quick action from the Gladstone government. Yet it must be conceded that when the Government declared for reform it moved along lines suggested by the Catholic bishops.

Catholic bishops in Ireland as well as in England agreed that Protestant ascendancy was the root cause of their problems. In 1868, Archbishop Manning told Gladstone that the existence of the Establishment "embitters every other question."[3] The vested interests of the Anglican Establishment became the pivotal point of Catholic attack, and made disendowment a necessary accompaniment to disestablishment. The situation had brought a working alliance between the English Liberation Society and the National Association of Ireland.

The National Association, originally organized by laymen and sanctioned by the clergy, had its birth early in 1865. In the beginning the Association had as its main object the abolition of the Irish Anglican Church Establishment. It later extended its agitation to include the land and education questions. The English Liberation Society of Nonconformists and Liberals stood ready to help the Irish Nationalists in their struggle for religious freedom. In April 1868, the National Association adopted a petition for disendowment, addressed to Parliament. By the time the Church question became practical politics in Parliament with Gladstone's resolutions, the Association had already decided on complete disendowment and secularization, and had given full support to the Liberal Party.

To the Liberal Party the Church question was of primary concern in Irish social reform. In dealing with the church question,

---

[3]The Dublin Review, Vol. 165, October, 1919, p. 170, "Irish Pages from the Postbags of Manning, Cullen & Gladstone," Archbishop Cullen to Mr. Gladstone, March 28, 1868.

however, the Government became inevitably involved with the other questions of land and university education as well. Certain aspects of disendowment touched on the land problem while both disestablishment and disendowment affected the university education question. If an end was to be put to the Irish Anglican Church Establishment, the position of the Dublin University was bound to be affected. The Irish Catholic bishops stressed the relationship between the Church and education questions in their reference to education as the factor on which the future welfare of their religion depended. In 1870, Gladstone expressly stated that the education question was to be dealt with "in the same spirit in which we have endeavoured to deal with the Church and Land in that country."[4] One statement from the priests shows how closely allied in their minds were the problems of Church, Land and University Education: "We will howl for your having other people's land as your own, if you will howl for uprooting every trace of Protestantism in our national education."[5]

Such pronouncements by the priests indicated that they were aware of the common element of Protestant ascendancy in ecclesiastical as well as educational affairs. In Ireland, as in England, Protestants dominated the wealth, land, and the professions. Not only was the great bulk of Irish land owned by Protestant landlords but the Anglican Establishment itself was richly endowed with large areas of land. Indeed, it was this fact which made disendowment such an important issue. In 1868, Gladstone was slow to perceive the importance of the land question. It was not until 1870 that the seriousness of that problem dawned on him. To others of his Cabinet, however, the land question was of supreme importance; among these was John Bright, President of the Board of Trade.

On May 21, 1869, Bright expressed this view in a letter to Gladstone:

> When the Irish Church question is out of the way, we shall find all Ireland, north and south

---

[4]Great Britain, 3 Hansard's Parliamentary Debates, cg(1870), 1132.

[5]"The Irish Land Question," Saturday Review, Vol. XXVIII (October, 1869), 527.

> alike, united in demanding something on the land
> question much broader than anything hitherto
> offered or proposed in compensation bills.[6]

During the middle 1860's, not only the Irish Catholic bishops but also the Irish Members of Parliament gave increasing attention to the land question viewing it as one surrounded by great difficulties. At their conference on December 5, 1865, the Irish members discussed the injustice of the Church Establishment, the land problem and university question. The Weekly Freeman's Journal reported that equality and no more was asked for; it also stated that "the land question occupied the first position in the minds of all."[7] In their resolutions the Irish members stated that they considered the land question "of paramount and pressing importance to the country."[8]

This emphasis on the land question increased more and more and had come well to the fore when the Liberals came to power in 1868. During discussions of the Church question on 1868 many voices stressed that the land, and not the Church, was at the root of Irish discontent. The Church question loomed forward, however, and until the summer of 1869, as Collison Black observed, "the question of land reform became secondary."[9] But this was not for long. In their Maynooth Resolutions of August 18, 1869, the Catholic bishops noted that the depressing discouragement of the people of Ireland, are at this period of their history, "to be attributed more to the want of a settlement of this question on fair and equitable principles than to any other cause."[10] They pressed for recognition of the rights of tenants as well as landowners.

---

[6]John Morley, *The Life of William Ewart Gladstone* (New York: the MacMillan Company, 1911), II, 282.

[7]*The Weekly Freeman's Journal*, December 16, 1865.

[8]*Ibid.*, December 9, 1865, p. 1

[9]Collison Black, *Economic Thought and the Irish Question, 1817-1870* (Cambridge: The University Press, 1960), p. 62.

[10]*Weekly Freeman's Journal*, 4 September 1869, p. 4 (Resolution X).

One of the biggest landowners in Ireland was the Anglican Church. It is true that the Catholic Church itself was becoming a vast landowner, and it was for this reason that Archbishop Cullen did not seem too enthusiastic over the land question in 1865. He could not ignore that question; but he spoke of it with the greatest caution, for he feared that if there were too many radical changes in the land arrangements of Ireland, the basis of property rights would be everywhere affected. By 1868, attacks on Papal temporal possessions were growing, while Catholics continued to harass the property of the Irish Anglican Church Establishment, which far surpassed that of the Catholic Church. John Bright had sensed the full implications of church ownership of land; therefore, in his proposals for land reform in 1868, he suggested that the experiments might be tried with the lands of the Irish Church, should they come under State control.

State action in Ireland was concerned largely with the problem of land tenure, a fundamental cause of the country's distress. Such action necessarily extended itself to Church property, and was feared by conservative men who strongly advocated private property. In May 1867, Sir John Gray, the Protestant proprietor of the Catholic Freeman's Journal and Liberal Member for Kilkenny, introduced a motion for complete disendowment of the Irish Church.[11] The plan was similar to that of John Stuart Mill in 1865. Mill, like Bright after him, suggested the creation of a peasant proprietary.

In 1865, the Dublin Review warned that any plan to introduce peasant proprietorship to a Parliament of landlords, would trigger an outcry about Communism."[12] The Catholic nierarchy in general gave their support to the plan, and in June 1868, Lord Malmesbury was quick to respond to Cardinal Manning's emphasis on joint-ownership in the land with the charge that it was "nothing but pure communism."[13] The Attorney General for Ireland, Mr. Chatterton, had also indicated in 1867 that the plan to redistribute

---

[11]Great Britain, 3 Hansard's Parliamentary Debates, CLXXXVII, 1867, p. 96.

[12]Dublin Review, Vol. V, New Series, October 1865, p. 473.

[13]Great Britain, 3 Hansard's Parliamentary Debates, CXCII, 1868, p. 2074.

Church property was "a direct approach to socialism and communism."[14] But State intervention in ecclesiastical matters was inevitable, and in 1868 the keynote of Gladstone's policy was secularization of property rather than concurrent endowment. This had great implications for the university question.

By concurrent endowment was meant the equal distribution of ecclesiastical property and State aid among competing religions according to their numerical proportions. Referred to as "levelling up" in the 1860's, it became a very important issue as the Liberals took over the reins of Government. Concurrent endowment affected the University question perhaps even more than it did the Church question. Both Gladstone and the Irish bishops rejected concurrent endowment although for different reasons. Gladstone felt that an end to concurrent endowment would also halt denominationalism in education. This would provide the State with the opportunity to consolidate its program of bringing about mixed education. The Catholic bishops, on the other hand, hoped that if concurrent endowment should be abolished, State control of their affairs would be considerably minimized and they could then carry forward without interference their program of denominational education. This difference in viewpoint on the same issue was to complicate the university education question to a great degree.

The university education question seemed the greatest threat of all. The Irish bishops, like Catholic bishops everywhere, placed the highest priority on having their people receive the kind of education which perfectly safeguarded their faith and morals. University education in Ireland for Catholics became more and more hopelessly removed from that goal. Indeed, the university education question in Ireland seemed to be the pivotal point around which much of the debate on higher education in nineteenth-century Britain revolved. In 1865, Archbishop Manning wrote to Cardinal Cullen asking him to require of the Government of England "justice to Catholics in the full sense, especially in education."[15] The Irish Catholic hierarchy became very much concerned about the

---

[14]Ibid., CLXXXVII, p. 131.

[15]Dublin Review, Vol. 165, Oct. 1919, p. 163, Archbishop Manning to Archbishop Cullen, Dec. 8, 1865.

proselytizing influence of the Protestant institutions. For this
reason the bishops considered the education question the most
urgent.

As in the case of the Church and land, Protestant ascendancy
to the Catholics was the root cause of the university education problem.
In a letter to the Right Honorable Thomas O'Hagan, the Irish
Attorney-General in 1863, Archbishop Cullen criticized the new
Board of Education which was reconstituted by Edward Cardwell, the
Chief Secretary of Ireland. Cullen pointed out that the Protestant
Government sought to exercise "complete control over the opinions
and teaching of the future Masters and Mistresses of the Catholic
children of Ireland."[16] The Catholic struggle against this was
expressed in their desire to intensify their efforts until they
should have a university comparable in its rights and privileges
to the Protestant universities. Educational **Equality** was at the core
of their wishes and demands.

For a long time the Irish Catholics were worried about inequality of educational opportunities. Degrees in medicine were
denied Catholic students who believed that their education should
be in the hands of their Church. Catholic law students were
unable to proceed to the bar with the same facility or rapidity
as Protestants if they did not obtain a degree. In England, however,
through the action of London University, Catholics enjoyed the
same equality with Protestants.

Inasmuch as the London University system had worked to the
satisfaction of Roman Catholics in England, Lord Wodehouse, Lord-
Lieutenant of Ireland in 1865, attempted to introduce the system
of affiliated colleges in Ireland. But by 1868, this was completely
unacceptable to the Irish Catholic hierarchy who sought equality through a
separate institution. It was this attitude in the bishops which
brought the principles of concurrent endowment and Voluntaryism
into sharp conflict with each other.

The Voluntary System or the free-will offerings of the faith-
ful had a five-fold purpose: (1) support of the bishops and paro-
chial clergy; (2) support of the regular clergy; (3) maintenance

---

[16]Patrick F. Moran, <u>The Pastoral Letters and Other Writings
of Cardinal Cullen</u> (Dublin: Browne and Nolan, 1882) II, p. 181.

of the churches; (4) maintenance of hospitals and charitable institutions; and (5) maintenance of Catholic schools and colleges. This system meant much to the Catholics. The staunch Catholic O'Neill Daunt noted with pride in his journal on July 26, 1869, "I preached the most out and out voluntaryism,"[17] which to him was a disovowal of the connection between Church and State, and a means of Catholic control of their own system of education in order to preserve the faith and morals of their youth. This desire to have separate education was in keeping with their demands for equality of educational opportunity, for to the Catholics, mixed education provided by the Establishment fostered inequality. Furthermore, in their grievances they argued that secondary education for Catholics was greatly neglected, and that the Protestant Endowed Schools were of greater advantage to the Establishment when it came to higher education. In 1866, Archbishop Cullen wrote to Sir George Grey, Irish Chief Secretary, emphasizing Catholic right to equality in education.[18]

Equality of educational opportunity was the pivot around which the principles of united or mixed education and denominational education were to be fought. Indeed educational equality had come to be closely identified with denominational education in Catholic thinking. Since Catholics had no way of obtaining legally recognized degrees, the Irish bishops feared that their youth would resort to Trinity College or to the Queen's University, both of which were frowned upon; it was for this reason that they sought a Charter for a Catholic University. The plan of Lord Mayo for a Catholic University in 1868 was built around this issue and was intended to satisfy Catholic demands. Mayo announced that such a university would stand in the same relation to the Roman Catholic population as Trinity College stood to the Protestant. Of course, this became a burning issue which was never settled on account of the extreme demands of the Catholics. These demands complicated the whole situation which Gladstone was to inherit.

---

[17] A Life Spent for Ireland, selections from the Journals of W.J. O'Neill Daunt edited by his daughter (London: T. Fisher Unwin, 1896), p. 262.

[18] Great Britain. Parliamentary Papers, 1866, LV p. 243. "Copies of Memorials addressed to the Secretary of State for the Home Department by Roman Catholic Prelates in Ireland, on the Subject of National and University Education in Ireland, and of the correspondence relating thereto," p. 5.

When Gladstone took office at the end of 1868, the university question, like the Church and land questions, was ripe for his attention. In March of that year he attempted to turn Catholic support away from the Mayo University plan to the Church question. This he did with the object of preventing the concession of the denominational principle for Irish university education. Insistence upon this principle was the cause of the cloudy atmosphere which surrounded Lord Mayo's scheme in 1868, and which presaged the difficulty that would envelop the university question in 1873 and the years after. Determined on the course of separate education, the Irish Catholic hierarchy held that the scheme of Lord Mayo did not go far enough. On the other hand, the Nonconformists thought it went too far. These dissenters were prepared to establish religious equality by depriving the Irish Church of any exclusive privileges which it enjoyed, but they were determined also to resist any attempt to create, at the cost or with the sanction of the State, any new sectarian institution. The bitter struggle which was to absorb the energies of both Liberal and Conservative parties for a dozen years was on.

Gladstone's positive commitment to this struggle was sparked by the Fenian explosion at Clerkenwell prison on December 13, 1867. The Fenian Brotherhood, or Irish Revolutionary Brotherhood, was established in America in 1858 by John O'Mahony. The movement sprang from the collapse of the Young Ireland movement. It is significant that the latter had been largely a literary and educational impulse, which appealed to young people to reform their country through education: "Educate that you may be free," was their watchword. The Young Ireland movement was a nationalist movement, and nationalists were denied equal educational opportunity; Young Irelandism also embodied the Church and land questions. Many priests were at one time members of the movement, including Dr. David Moriarty, Bishop of Kerry, who was to play a prominent role in the fight for university reform in Ireland. Throughout its active period, Young Ireland did not fail to identify Irish nationalism with the land question.

Irish nationalism and independence was also the goal of the Fenians, but they had different motives and employed other means of action. They took their names from the ancient warriors of Ireland and set out to procure by terror and force what the peaceful agitators had failed to obtain. Indeed, force to them was the only effective weapon for overthrowing English rule and establishing the Irish Republic. Because of this, their role in the struggle for higher education reform was only an indirect one. It is true that the leaders of the movement were intellectuals, but the followers were almost exclusively composed of young men of the lower classes in town and country who were mainly interested in violent activities. The Fenians were indifferent to religion. On May 27, 1867, Lord Granville, in a speech on the second reading in the House of Lords of the Habeas Corpus Suspension (Ireland) Act Continuance Bill, argued that "Fenianism had no wish to remodel the Irish Church,... and it was also true that it had no care for the land tenure question."[19] In general, the Catholic clergy withheld their support, holding fast to the traditional teaching of the Catholic Church against all forms of rebellion.

The so-called Fenian rebellion of 1867 was a complete disaster. On the whole, Fenianism lacked tangible success, yet it had not totally failed; its underground influence continued to be felt more and more, and indirectly, by remaining a disquieting feature, it was bound to draw attention to Irish conditions. The Fenian amnesty movement was a great revelation of the deep sympathy which was felt for the few uncompromising and self-sacrificing members; and, ironically, it was the Fenian outrage at Clerkenwell which commanded the attention of Gladstone, bringing forth speedily his policy of reform in the Irish Church, land, and university education, which was to aim at satisfying the Catholic bishops who had condemned Fenianism.

If the threat of Fenianism meant something to Gladstone in stimulating in him a fresh awakening of the seriousness of Irish social conditions in general, it was also of great import to Cardinal Manning in connection with the education question in particular. Manning, Head of the Roman Catholic Church in England, wrote to Gladstone in 1868, appealing to him "not to diminish the possibility" of the Disraeli Government's plan for Irish University education. This appeal was based on the belief that putting Irish education into the hands of the Catholic Church was the only way of keeping Ireland from anarchy.[20] This reference was to Fenianism; Manning's statement implied the indirect impact of Fenianism as well as the overall importance of the university education question.

---

[19]Great Britain, 3 <u>Hansard's Parliamentary Debates</u>, 1867, CLXXXVII, p. 1122.

[20]Gladstone Papers, B. M. Add. MS: 44249, f. 26. Manning to Gladstone, March 11, 1868, as referred to by E. R. Norman, <u>The Catholic Church and Ireland in The Age of Rebellion, 1859-1873</u> (New York: Cornell University Press, 1965), p. 265.

But Gladstone was already aware of the dangers of Fenianism to Irish society. Truly, it was the sharp realization of that threat which convinced him that the Government's university education measure was futile. His reply to Manning indicated that he could never support what he considered a hopeless scheme for endowing a denominational university out of the Consolidated fund. Gladstone's reply reflected the turn his actions would take in his treatment of the university question.

By 1868, the university question became the sore point between Liberal Catholicism and Ultramontanism in Ireland. It will be remembered that the Catholic clergy argued for the voluntary system in preference to concurrent endowment. Yet there were some Irish Catholics, prominent among them being Bishop Moriarty of Kerry, and Aubrey De Vere, a convert of Limerick, who desired State aid for education. The arguments surrounding proposals for concurrent endowment largely colored the Irish Catholic discussion of the Church question up to 1868. In that year, Dr. C. W. Russell, President of Maynooth, extended the matter to the university question, when he wrote in vain to Gladstone urging him to consider Maynooth College as an educational rather than as an ecclesiastical case for the purpose of endowment.

The battle over the principle of endowment was to be fought over the Church question, but it was clear in 1868 that Gladstone and the Liberals intended to link it with educational grants too. It might be assumed that Gladstone and the Liberals underestimated the strength of the ecclesiastical position of the Ultramontanes as they approached the problems of Church reform and university education. For while the Liberal Party was planning to disestablish the Irish Anglican Church, the essence of Cullen's ecclesiastical policy was to strengthen the authority of the Roman Catholic Church in Ireland. To Cullen, the role of education as one of the prime means for accomplishing this, was not to be minimised.

Everywhere it was conceived that the ecclesiastical organization of the Church of Rome was a most powerful society, and wherever it ran counter to temporal interests, serious problems nearly always developed. In Europe, struggles between Church and State had nearly always been precipitated by the educational claims of the Catholic hierarchies. This was no less true of Ireland; the Irish bishops' educational demands were first publicly announced in 1859, and until 1863, education was more or less the sole issue deliberated upon. It was only after 1864 that the hierarchy included the Church and land questions and agitated for their solution concurrently. Four years later, in a debate on the state of Ireland in 1868, initiated by J. F. Maguire, Liberal Member of Parliament for Cork City, C. N. Newdgate, Member of Parliament for Warwickshire, declared that the danger of Ultramontanism in these matters rested "with Dr. Cullen at the head of the Roman Catholic hierarchy in Ireland."[21] This observation had special significance for the university question which was to bring the most severe strain to bear on the government.

The new government was liberal, but its liberalism was tempered by conservatism, which was evidenced by the stand taken by Gladstone, who, while disposed to help the Irish, was in no way prepared to let them have all their demands in educational matters. Indeed, he did not always show a keen desire to champion the cause of the Irish. In 1853, as Chancellor of the Exchequer, he imposed on the Irish the Income Tax which Peel had withheld a decade before, and this the Irish members remembered quite well. On March 28, 1865, during the House of Commons debate on the Anglican Church Establishment in Ireland, Gladstone refused to admit the charges that were laid against the Anglican Church, stating vigorously that "it is my belief that the Irish (Anglican) Church is perfectly free from such abuses."[22]

Earlier, however, Gladstone did show some concern for Irish social conditions. As he travelled on the continent in 1845, Gladstone held conversations with European statesmen and was quite moved by their view of the English treatment of Ireland. One of his letters to Mrs. Gladstone, on the eve of his return from Germany, indicates his deep concern for Ireland. With great feeling he wrote:

> Ireland! Ireland! that cloud in the west, that coming storm, the minister of God's retribution upon cruel and inverterate and but half-atoned injustice! Ireland forces upon us those great social and great religious questions-- God grant that we may have courage to look them in the face and to work through them.[23]

---

[21]Great Britain, 3 Hansard's Parliamentary Debates, CXC (1868), p. 1639.

[22]Great Britain, 3 Hansard's Parliamentary Debates, CLXXXVIII (1865), p. 420.

[23]Tilney Basset (ed.), Gladstone to His Wife (London: Methuen & Co. Ltd., 1936), p. 64.

It seems then that Gladstone was divided in his attitude toward Ireland. John Morley speaks of "that division of sensibility between the demands of spiritual and secular life which remained throughout one of the marked traits of his career."[24] Gladstone was himself a devout and sincere Churchman; he loved the Church; at the same time he wanted to do justice to Ireland by disestablishing the Irish Church. Likewise, in educational matters, he was as equally divided. Dr. C. W. Russell, President of Maynooth College, could recall a conversation with Gladstone in which the latter admitted that although he considered the Irish Catholics wrong about education, he also realized that they had a right to their demands. But although Gladstone had never desired a Charter for a Catholic university, he might have agreed to one anyway if it were not for the policy of endowment, for he had great sympathy for the Roman Catholic grievance in respect to higher education.

The higher education difficulty in Ireland was further heightened by anti-Catholic feeling in England. From time to time the Catholic bishops kept up their demand for a Chartered Catholic college or university. The British Government at times tried to make concessions, but these were often accompanied by outbursts of Protestant opposition. In August, 1865, H. A. Bruce, Vice President of the Privy Council for Education, submitted unofficially and without guarantee of their adoption, proposals for a Royal Irish University to the Catholic bishops who were meeting in Dublin. The fourth proposal stated that in addition to the six Government nominees constituting the thirty-two member Senate, six members shall be selected at first, and ever after from the religious bodies in the following proportions, namely, three Roman Catholic prelates, two prelates of the Established Church, and one member from the Synod of Ulster. The plan was later endorsed by Lord Wodehouse in a speech delivered on the occasion of the annual meeting of the Queen's University. One important aspect of that speech was Wodehouse's admission that respect must be paid to Catholic conscientious objections to the mixed principle.[25]

Protestant opposition to the Government's proposal was stepped up and the press in general fanned the flames by pointing to the plan as a triumph of ultramontanism. The view was taken that the Government was forced into conciliation by a small group of members from the National Association following the election of 1865. The Times

---

[24] John Morley, op.cit. I, p. 81.

[25] The Times, October 16, 1865, p. 8.

stated that "notwithstanding all Lord Wodehouse says in favour of mixed education it is becoming only too manifest that the result of the long conflict between denominational and mixed education is to be decided in favour of the former."[26]

Public opinion was further outraged later in 1865 by the extreme actions of certain Roman Catholic priests. Notably among these was Bishop Patrick Dorrian of Down and Connor, who was bent on having episcopal control and supervision of the Catholic Institute in Belfast. In 1867, Lord Claude Hamilton made bitter reference to that episode during a debate in the House of Commons on the Established Church. He expressed Protestant fears of ultramontane education when he asked whether they were prepared to "destroy the Established Church in Ireland in order that such mandates might come into force."[27] All this reflects the inherent conflict between denominational and mixed education, which was bound to be accentuated by disestablishment.

It is not surprising, therefore, that the Dublin Protestants were very critical of Gladstone's proposal to disestablish the Irish Church, declaring that the Royal Supremacy was the only obstacle to the establishment of the Pope as the supreme ruler in Ireland. Of greater concern to Gladstone was the opposition of some leading Catholics, although the important step in disestablishing the Irish Church was being taken in their behalf. Despite this concession, many Catholics were angry at the elaborate arrangement which seemed to prevent them from recovering any of their cathedrals. Others considered the capitalization plan a re-endowment of Protestantism, and concluded that this was anything but religious equality. Many prominent Catholics such as O'Neill Daunt, who brought Cullen into the Liberal alliance, had even come to distrust Gladstone.

Notwithstanding the momentous issues, climates of opinion, and complications of the situation facing him, Gladstone braced himself for the task; in fact, he seemed anxious to tackle the problem. On April 11, 1868, he wrote to Lord Granville stating that for some years he had been "watching the sky with a strong sense of the obligation to act with the first streak of dawn."[28] They were difficult questions, and

---

[26] The Times, October 16, 1865, p. 8.

[27] Great Britain, 3 Hansard's Parliamentary Debates. CLXXXVII, 1867, p. 175.

[28] Phillip Magnus, Gladstone: A Biography (London: John Murray, 1954), p. 196.

it was left for time to reveal the full extent of the step his Government was about to take. Surely, the university question would not be resolved at the end of the Liberals' term of office in 1874, and the Conservatives would continue the search for a solution for the next six years. The Catholics had great hope in disestablishment as an avenue to solve the university question. Cardinal Cullen expressed this as he referred to the forthcoming Irish Church Act, in an address to the Historical Society of the Catholic University in 1868:

> And when this great origin of the evils that afflict us shall have been removed, we may hope for better days, and be confident that the claims of this Catholic University will be admitted.[29]

---

[29]P. F. Moran, op. cit. III, p. 185.

CHAPTER II

THE CHURCH QUESTION

The religious establishment in Ireland was one of the general results of the Reformation. In certain parts of Europe, Catholicism remained triumphant and it continued to be the state religion, while in other areas, Protestantism was established by the states in which its forms prevailed. Thus, in England during the sixteenth century, the acts of uniformity established the Episcopal or Anglican Church as the people's faith, subordinate to and protected by the government, and supported by assigned revenues. The Episcopal Church was also established in Ireland by the English as the Church of Ireland similarly protected by the government, and supported by property allotted to it. This Church was established for the expressed purpose of promoting the English cause and converting Catholics to the Anglican faith. It was indeed a symbol of alien domination, for it represented the supremacy of the few and the subjection of the many.

In spite of these efforts, the Episcopalian Church failed to win to itself many of the Catholics, the result being that in Ireland where most of the people were Catholics, only a few possessed privilege and power in Church and State affairs. The members of the Established Church, in 1861, numbered only about seven hundred thousand, or approximately one-eighth of the total population of almost six million. A fair number of Anglicans resided in Dublin or near the coast, but in many Catholic districts there were just a few Church members to several Anglican benefices, and indeed some had only one member apiece. Yet, the Church possessed a net revenue of more than six hundred pounds sterling. A small minority of the people in Ireland, and the most prosperous ones too, received a large annual subsidy while the remaining inhabitants had to provide for their religion in whatever way they could. It is true that there were worse times when Catholics and Dissenters, in addition to supporting their own religions, were forced to contribute to the upkeep of the Anglican system. Nevertheless, by the end of the 1860's the established and endowed Church of Ireland, in the minds of a great many people, was the number one grievance among the Irish Catholics.

One of the prime factors in this grievance was proselytism. The Protestant Church widely engaged in various kinds of proselytizing activities through relief programs in famine areas, or at times by threat of eviction from the land. But it was educational proselytism that was most systematically organized and assiduously carried out, and it was this the Catholics feared most. Again and again, the Catholic hierarchy assailed Protestant bishops as the keenest supporters of proselytism not only in their missionary activities, but also in the National Schools. Of course, it hardly needs to be pointed out that the Catholics themselves were also charged with practicing proselytism; the case of young Edgar Mortara, who was born of Jewish family but was removed from his parents and brought up in the Catholic religion, is an outstanding example. Notwithstanding, the Catholics continued to point to their disadvantages. In 1859, the Dublin Review noted that the motives behind the conversion of hundreds of children of Catholic parents were those of terror and profit to set a premium upon the profession of Protestantism.[1]

The bastion of Protestantism was even further bulwarked through Protestant control of higher education. Trinity College, the wealthy Protestant institution, was founded in the reign of Elizabeth, and was exclusively controlled by members of the Irish Church. For a long time, therefore, Protestant ascendancy was secured at Trinity College by reserving privleges, honors, and even admission, for members of the Established Church. Religious tests were imposed, and fellowships and foundation scholarships were closed to those who did not profess the religion of the Establishment. In 1843, Denis Caulfield Heron, a Roman Catholic student, who competed for a scholarship, was declared entitled to election after the examination results were revealed. However, since he declined to take the usual Protestant oath, he was denied the scholarship. It was held that the Act of 1793 which threw open the degrees of Trinity College to members of other religious bodies did not give Roman Catholics the right to become members of this corporation. It was not until 1854 that the College Board, under heavy criticisms, created non-foundation scholarships equal in value to those on the foundation for those students who refused to take the required test. Religious inequality had become identified with educational inequality.

---

[1] Dublin Review, June 1859, Vol. 46, p. 427.

Perhaps, the area which most clearly revealed religious inequality and consequently educational inequality was that of endowment. The Anglican Church in Ireland was well endowed; in 1868, its annual income was approximately ₤613,984. The landed property of the Church was ₤229,000 per year from rents paid by 10,000 tenants, distributed over 900 estates, "scattered over the whole of Ireland."[2] The Church's capital was, accordingly, about ₤16,000,000. Its dignitaries were rich and many idle; excessive wealth even led to abuses. At the close of the eighteenth century and during much of the nineteenth, the Anglican Church remained supreme in Ireland. This was the Church of the ruling minority and England's first line of defence in Ireland. Filled with the plunder of the confiscations and rich with the spoils of the Church of Rome, the Irish Church had continued to exact its annual revenue of tithes from Catholic peasants. All this was a terrible burden to Catholics who looked upon the Establishment as the emblem and instrument of English rule, of injustice and inequality.

Like the Irish Anglican Church Establishment, Trinity College or Dublin University was richly endowed. The value of the property which Trinity College received from the State at various times may be estimated at ₤30,000 per annum, plus an additional 6,000 or ₤7,000 a year from private estate. Dividends, interests, and receipts from students amounted to about ₤20,000. The gross total income for the year 1888 was ₤62,563. 15^s. 10d.[3] Its resources from time to time were increased by frequent grants and donations from the State until it became reputed as the richest college in Europe; hence, the college became an exclusively Protestant place of learning, and thus, the interests of the Anglican Church were safely guarded. This was a reflection of what the Church stood for at various times. It was, for instance, very High Church during the reigns of the last two Stuarts and Queen Anne, and Low Church during the time of Walpole. The Church of Ireland was strongly devoted to the college and the union between Church and State gave it the right to determine educational policy.

---

[2] Great Britain, **Parliamentary Papers**, 1881, XXVIII, 63 "Report of the Church Temporalities in Ireland for the period 1869-1880," p. 7.

[3] Great Britain, **Parliamentary Papers**, 1889, LIX, 389, "Trinity College, Dublin: Return showing the Gross and Net Revenues for the year 1888," p. 3.

The Church-State relationship which existed in England from Reformation times also held true in Ireland. The Reformation Parliament of 1536 had declared Henry VIII supreme head on earth of the Church of Ireland. Throughout the centuries, the English sovereign remained head of the Irish Church, but in 1800, the Church of Ireland and the Church of England were legally united by the Act of Union. From time to time Catholics suffered many disabilities: they were denied civil rights, could not acquire land, nor serve in the army; they could not even vote prior to the Catholic Emancipation Act of 1829. For many years in Ireland, no man was permitted openly to have the advantages of learning unless he was a Protestant. The Penal Laws prohibited Catholics from keeping school or teaching children other than their own, or even from sending their children abroad to be educated. In the realm of higher education, the State for a long time cooperated with the Church in preventing Catholics from getting a proper education. Indeed, the Church-State relationship became well consolidated, carrying within itself serious consequences for Catholic higher education. For instance, when the Irish Parliament passed a great measure of relief in 1793, making Catholics eligible for degrees and minor prizes from Trinity College, the Protestant statutes of the college made that impossible. It was because of these things that the Catholics welcomed disestablishment of the Irish Church in addition to wanting their own chartered university.

The Irish Catholics were not satisfied with Maynooth College. This college might be considered somewhat of a counterpart to Trinity College, Dublin. It was established in 1796 on the proposal of Ulster Protestants for a Catholic college whereby Irish priests could be educated at home. The college was endowed by the State with the equivalent of ₤9,000 per annum, raised to ₤26,000 per year in 1845. As a State institution, the Maynooth College was much less endowed than Trinity College although it served a larger population. This aroused strong feeling against the Establishment, and many Irish Catholics agitated for disestablishment and disendowment. Some felt that disestablishment would diminish the threat of proselytism as well as induce less state interference, while others saw in disendowment a better chance of equal distribution of state funds. Archbishop Cullen had suggested in 1864 that the Anglican Church property should be sold, and the amount placed into the hands of a Commission to be applied for public purposes, such as building schools and colleges. Gladstone confirmed this view in 1868, when he presented his motion in the Commons calling for an end to the Establishment. But while Gladstone agreed to a residue fund for the benefit of Ireland, he specifically called for putting "an end within the realm to all Grants from the Consolidated Fund to be applied for purposes of any religious denomination whatever."[4] Of course, the Catholics would have no quarrel with this until they realized that Gladstone would apply the principle to religious education as well.

If Ireland would benefit from disestablishment and disendowment, the Catholics were somewhat divided in their views as to exactly how this would occur. All agreed that Maynooth College was inextricably bound up with the Church question. But while some argued for the Voluntary principle, others pressed for continued State assistance. It is true that the Voluntary principle was more immediately applicable to the churches, but it was often extended to schools and colleges. Some Irish Catholics, backed by supporters of the English Liberation Society, urged that unless the Maynooth grant was relinquished, the disestablishment question was imperiled. On the other hand, the leaders at Maynooth advocated that the College be treated as an educational rather than an ecclesiastical establishment, in which case the endowment would be continued after the Irish Church was disestablished.

For this reason, the Irish bishops declared for disestablishment and secularization of Church property. The bishops hoped that their cause for education could be helped by the State's application of Irish ecclesiastical property. The National Association, too, was in favor of complete disendowment and secularization. On April 10, 1868, the Association's Committee report on the Church question demanded disestablishment and disendowment, suggesting that the revenues of the Irish Church be made into an Irish fund for secular purposes, other than "to relieve property from the charges upon it for the relief of the poor."[5]

Gladstone was also in favor of secularization. He was, therefore, in accord with the Catholics on this point with regard to the Church question, although it is conceivable that the Catholics had

---

[4]Great Britain, 3 Hansard's Parliamentary Debates, CXCL, 1868, p. 472.

[5]The Times, April 10, 1868, p. 8.

religious education in mind as one of the "other purposes" for which the Irish fund should be used. Indeed, this would become the center of disagreement when it came to the education question. Aubrey de Vere, in 1867, had prophesied the evil effects politically and socially generated by secularization, "a course," he said, "which far from retrieving the injustice of centuries, rendered such a retrieval at any future time impossible."[6]

Aubrey de Vere was concerned with secularization from the standpoint of the redistribution of Church funds, as he expressed in his pamphlet entitled "The Church Settlement of Ireland" in 1867.[7] More important, however, the principle of secularization stemming from disestablishment had great significance for the university question. For Gladstone would insist that the secularized funds from the disestablished Church be used to promote secular education. This insistence on united secular education would meet opposition from the Catholics, who, once disestablishment was over, would continue to demand denominational education. Surely, Catholic interest in secularization was merely for a diversion of State funds from Protestant use to achieve their denominational education objectives.

For the time being, however, Gladstone fully realized not only Catholic dissatisfaction with the Irish Church Establishment, but also the extent to which the problems of higher education were intertwined with those of the Church. So firm was this realization, that in March, 1868, Gladstone embarked on turning Catholic support from the Mayo university plan toward the plan for disestablishment. It is true that this step was dictated by the need to avoid conceding to the denominational principle in Irish higher education. In 1868, he addressed the electors of southwest Lancashire with this statement: "We refused to open a new source of discord through the establishment by the State of any denominational university. We repudiate the policy of universal endowment."[8] But Gladstone also knew very well that disestablishment would greatly appeal to the Catholics, as their complaints against the educational

---

[6]*Recollections of Aubrey de Vere* (New York: E. Arnold, 1897) p. 334.

[7]*Ibid*.

[8]W. E. Gladstone, *Speeches in Southwest Lancashire, October, 1868* (Liverpool: Egerton Smith and Co., 1868), p. iv.

system involved the Establishment to a very large extent. It was with fairly rapid ease that the Irish bishops shifted from the Mayo plan for a Catholic university to the Church question.

Mayo's proposal for a Catholic university did intend to give the Catholics reasonable control. In a statement on this matter, Lord Mayo announced that "to the university thus constituted ... utmost freedom should be given, the only condition made being that...no student of another faith should be required to attend any Catholic religious observance."[9] But the Disraeli Government insisted on a lay governing body, and the bishops objected to this as the letter to Lord Mayo presented by Patrick Leahy, Archbishop of Cashel and John Derry, Bishop of Clonfert, revealed.[10] Mayo indicated the incompatibility between the episcopal and governmental views in his reply that the proposals made in their letter would strike at the very root of the principles that were being laid down, and that their recommendations "could not be entertained."[11] Early in March, 1868, Disraeli wrote to the Queen informing her that "it is doubtful whether the R. C. prelates will accept our offer."[12] Certainly the bishops rejected the plan as they did not feel very secure with a lay governing body. Cullen's letter to Manning revealed that some Catholic laymen were viewed with as much distrust as the Protestants themselves:

> It would be also important to know how the laymen are to be chosen. We have some laymen in Ireland who are as hostile to the rights of the Church as our open enemies. Probably the choice of Government would fall upon men of

---

[9] Great Britain, Parliamentary Papers, 1867-68, LIII, 779, "Correspondence relative to the Proposed Charter to a Roman Catholic University in Ireland," p. 8.

[10] Ibid., Leahy and Derry to Mayo, March 31, 1869.

[11] Ibid.

[12] George Buckle, The Letters of Queen Victoria, 1862-1885, Vol. I, p. 510, Disraeli to the Queen, March 4, 1868.

that class, in which case the education of the country, would not at all be safe.[13]

Perhaps the bishops' objection to the Government's suggestion for lay control stemmed from their experience with the governing procedures at Maynooth College. By the 1795 Act of the Irish Parliament which established that College, all the rules and statutes received the approval of the Protestant Lord Lieutenant before becoming effective. Hence, the Catholics did not have autonomy over the college which trained their own priests; yet this is what they wanted so much. They were also greatly concerned about the State's perogative to send commissions of inquiry into the college. In 1855, the Harrowby Commission carried out an investigation at Maynooth, and closely interrogated several professors concerning the use of de Ligouri's texts which made allowance for equivocation in some oath-taking cases. Bishop Furlong admitted that Ligouri's theology was what he "principally referred to."[14] However, all Catholics did not practice it in relation to their constitutional oaths. Many Catholics preferred not to take an oath abjuring their beliefs for the sake of being protected by the Constitution.

Oath taking was another sore point in the relationship between the Irish hierarchy and the Establishment. It caused great irritation in Ireland, and might even have added more bitterness to the higher education problem. For not only were office-holders in Ireland required to take oaths, but students at Maynooth as well. In 1865, William Monsell, speaking before the Committee to consider the Roman Catholic Oath Bill, drew attention to the humiliation and frustration of prominent Catholics who not only had to condemn their own religion, but were bound to declare that they "abjure any intention to subvert the present Church Establishment...or weaken the Protestant

---

[13]Manning Papers, Cullen to Manning, March 11, 1868, as quoted by E. R. Norman, <u>The Catholic Church and Ireland in the Age of Rebellion, 1859-1873</u>, p. 265.

[14]Great Britain, <u>Parliamentary Papers</u>, 1855, XXII, 1 "Commission for Inquiring into the Mangement and Government of the College of Maynooth," Minutes of Evidence, p. 91.

Religion or Protestant Government in the United Kingdom."[15] Many Catholics had even come to question the integrity of Maynooth priests, blaming it largely on the oath. Some priests were often suspected of leaning toward the English cause. The outcry among Catholics caught the attention of the Chief Secretary, Chichester Fortescue, who, on April 30, 1866, announced the appointment of a Commission to inquire into oath-taking by Irish officers and the Maynooth students.

The Oath Commission was quite sympathetic to the Catholic case and recommended that the oath of allegiance for students, officers, and servants at Maynooth be retained, but that it should be altered in form.[16] In 1868, a bill was passed, after some difficulty, implementing the main lines of the report. Its provisions greatly reduced the number of persons taking oaths. In Ireland, only a few persons were required to take oaths, chief among them being the Lord Lieutenant, the Lord Chancellor, and the Commander of the Forces and the Chief Secretary.[17] Earl Grey had perceived some relationship betweem oath-taking and the Establishment. When a bill aimed at modifying the oaths taken by Catholics failed to pass the House of Lords in 1865, he warned that the oaths would not stop the struggle to end the Establishment, but rather that "the rejection of this Bill would only accelerate that struggle."[18]

Grey was correct in his assumption that the struggle for disestablishment would intensify. At the center of that struggle was the university question, and the immediate spark was provided by the problems surrounding the Mayo plan. Gladstone's resolutions on the Irish Church in March, 1868, strongly appealed to the Catholics; actually, the Irish Catholic bishops, for the moment at least, turned away from the Charter and concentrated on the Established Church, for they had been disappointed with Disraeli and the Mayo Catholic University plan. Cardinal Manning confessed, "I have felt that a ravine, I will not say a gulf, opened between us when the Resolutions on the Irish Church were laid upon the

---

[15] Great Britian, 3 Hansard's Parliamentary Debates, 1865, CLXXVIII, p. 28.

[16] Great Britain, Parliamentary Papers, 1867, XXXI, 40, "Report of the Oaths Commission."

[17] Great Britain, Parliamentary Papers, 1867-68, IV, Bill 113, "Promissory Oaths Act," p. 7.

[18] Annual Register, 1865, p. 92.

table of the House," as he wrote to Disraeli on December 2, 1868.[19] Commenting on this, Monypenny and Buckle stated that "whatever the degree of Manning's responsibility, the facts and dates suggest that the Roman Catholic authorities were diverted from adhesion to Disraeli's programme by Gladstone's superior bid."[20]

After all, the bishops knew very well that the Church Establishment was the root cause of their educational problems. They were quite impressed with Gladstone's determination that in order to reach a settlement of the question of the Irish Church "that Church, as a State Church, must cease to exist."[21] They were equally impressed by Gladstone's further statement that "if we are prepared to take those decisive measures with respect to the Church of Ireland which have been recommended, it is plain that the position of the National University would require to be specially considered."[22] This reference was to Trinity College, and it reveals the close relationship between the Church and university questions, which might have raised the bishops' hopes for a solution to the university problem.

But the bishops had miscalculated the implications of disestablishment for Catholic higher education objectives. In this regard, Monypenny and Buckle state that, as a result of disestablishment "they got nothing of the Church revenues, nor even, till after forty years, the Catholic University which was within their grasp."[23] Moreover, Gladstone's reasons for wanting to bring about disestablishment were not the same as those of the Catholic bishops. Gladstone disapproved of the Mayo plan for a Catholic University on the grounds that it carried within it the seeds of denominational education. He could not agree, therefore, to endow a Catholic university out of the Consolidated Fund, for the goal of the Liberals was united education which the Catholics despised.

---

[19]W. F. Monypenny and G. E. Buckle, The Life of Benjamin Disraeli (New York: The Macmillan Company, 1929), II, p. 350.

[20]Ibid.

[21]Great Britian, 3 Hansard's Parliamentary Debates, CXC, 1868, p. 1764.

[22]Ibid., pp. 1754-55.

[23]Monypenny and Buckle, op.cit., II, p. 350.

Cardinal Cullen and the Catholic bishops became more and more aware of the educational objectives of the Liberals, they correctly assumed that their hopes in education might be disappointed. However, it was not without hope for the eventual success of the Charter plan, that the Catholics supported the Liberals on disestablishment. This they did, despite the concensus that Gladstone was further from the Catholic view than Disraeli, and would never accede to the full demands of the bishops, as Disraeli was inclined to do. In April, 1867, the Dublin Review noted that Catholic principles differed far less from those of the Conservatives than from those of the Liberals, and that a Catholic might even try "to make political capital out of the Liberalism which he detests."[24] All this shows the tremendous importance the Catholics attached to disestablishment.

The disestablishment of the Irish Church was first among Gladstone's election promises, and he lost no time in embarking on it when he assumed office. As the Commons met in Committee on March 1, 1869, he moved leave to bring in the Irish Church Bill "to put an end to the Establishment of the Church of Ireland and to make provision in respect of the temporalities thereof and in respect of the Royal College of Maynooth."[25] Many Catholics were not happy with the bill because it threatened the disendowment of Maynooth College. In this can be seen the close link between the church and university questions. The Maynooth clause stipulated, among other things, that the Catholic College of Maynooth would not receive any further State aid, although it would be compensated with an amount fourteen times the annual grant.[26] The Catholics wished that the State grant be continued for educational purposes but not for religious purposes, for they preferred the voluntary principle to concurrent endowment for their churches. During the Commons Committee discussion on the Maynooth grant, T. O'Conor Don, Member of Parliament for Roscommon, represented the Catholics; he ended the long debate between Gladstone and the Irish Catholics by claiming, like Dr. Russell, Maynooth's president, that the question of the Maynooth endowment was more largely educational than religious.[27]

---

[24]Dublin Review, Vol. 8, new series, April 1867, p. 385.

[25]Great Britain, 3 Hansard's Parliamentary Debates, CXCIV (1869), p. 412.

[26]Great Britain, Parliamentary Papers, 1869, III, 85, "Irish Church Bill," p. 19.

[27]Great Britain, 3 Hansard's Parliamentary Debates, CXCVI (1869), p. 146.

In the minds of many English Radicals and Dissenters, however, the Catholics were holding this line to further their aims of State supported denominational education. Having discovered that the Radicals and Dissenters were opposed to the continuation of the Maynooth grant, Gladstone took sides with them against the Irish Catholics. The Maynooth grant was always very significant to Gladstone with regard to the Establishment. In the Chapter of Autobiography, he described it as "a testing question for the foundations of the Irish Established Church."[28] Indeed, the Maynooth grant, which was objected to by many Protestants seemed a standing contradiction to the Establishment. The Irish Church Act of 1869 provided that the Maynooth grant would cease with disestablishment which was to be effective on January 1, 1871.[29] The Irish Reqium Donum, a comparable State endowment to the Presbyterian Church, was also abolished. On the other hand, Trinity College, by the Irish Church Act, received £122,000 in compensation for the loss of the eighteen advowsons granted to it by letters patent in 1610.

But Trinity College was not specially addressed by the Irish Church Act of 1869. However, so close was the relationship between the Church and university questions in the minds of Gladstone and other leaders that mention of Trinity College was inevitable. In a discussion in the House of Commons in May, 1869, T. O'Connor Don reminded the members that "though Trinity College was not in the Bill, yet the case of that College was postponed, not decided."[30] Gladstone was very anxious to do something about the endowment of Trinity College, so on March 29, he wrote to Chichester Fortescue on the Maynooth compensation, and made the following reference to Trinity College:

> I should be glad to know whether we could
> now take in hand the framing of a measure
> with regard to Trinity College...I conclude

---

[28]William Ewart Gladstone, <u>Chapter of Autobiography</u> (London: J. Murray, 1868), p. 26.

[29]Great Britain, <u>Parliamentary Papers</u>, Vol. III (1868-1869), Bill 27 for the full text of the Provisions of the Irish Church Act.

[30]Great Britain, 3 <u>Hansard's Parliamentary Debates</u>, CXCVI, 1869, p. 146.

we should neutralize the University and seize
on its behalf a large part of the endowments,
leaving to the College as a denominational
institution a portion of them for its own
purposes.[31]

Gladstone also recognized the right of an institution to pursue denominational education, although he was quite opposed to State endowment of that principle: Consequently, Gladstone rejected concurrent endowment with regard to the Church question, thereby signalling the line of action he would take on the same issue in the university question. When he introduced his resolutions on the Irish Church in May, 1868, Gladstone intended to put an end to concurrent endowment not only of churches but universities as well. The Irish Catholics agreed with him, but not completely. They desired concurrent endowment for education, but not for churches. Gladstone acted in harmony with Liberal persuasion that united secular education was preferable to the old system of State endowment and religious inequality. But such a course was sure to intensify the degree of polarization between the Irish hierarchy and the English Liberals, and to increase the difficulties which beset the university question. For the problem involving the endowment of Maynooth, which Gladstone denied, was to remain a thorn in the relationship between him and the Catholics.

The Catholics gained new strength and courage from disestablishment for their continued efforts at a settlement of the university question. Immediately after the passage of the Irish Church Act of 1869, the National Association declared the necessity of following this up with action aimed at a solution of educational problems. In 1872, Thomas Pope, a priest of the archdiocese of Dublin, noted that after the disestablishment of the Protestant Church the "nation is now aroused to the most vigorous efforts"[32] to obtain a system of education based on religious freedom. On July 4, 1871, the Nenagh Town Commissioners passed a resolution appointing James Hanly, Esq.,

---

[31] Carlingford Papers, CP 1/41, Gladstone to Fortescue, March 29, 1869, as quoted by Eric Norman, The Catholic Church and Ireland in the Age of Rebellion, 1859-1873, p. 373.

[32] Thomas Pope, The Council of the Vatican and the Events of the Times (Boston: Patrick Donahoe, 1872), p. 223.

as magistrate chairman to represent Nenagh on the deputation from the Irish Corporations; they were to meet with Mr. Gladstone to urge that Catholics were entitled to the same privileges as Protestants with respect to primary, intermediate and university education.[33]

In general, while Catholic interest in education included all levels of education, the prime target of the hierarchy continued to be higher education. The Catholic bishops, upset over the cessation of the Maynooth grant stipulated by the Church Act, issued their Maynooth Resolutions demanding a portion of the funds which were set aside for the royal endowed schools. They soon widened their demands with emphasis on the university question. The bishops declared that the Ministers of Government must know that they "demand for Irish Catholics, Catholic education," since "it alone can be in keeping with the feelings of the vast majority of the nation."[34] At Maynooth, they condemned mixed education and called upon both clergy and laity to use every possible means constitutionally to oppose the mixed system.

For many years the Irish Catholic hierarchy declared against the mixed system which was the main feature of the national system of education; and the national system was maintained by the Establishment. The Catholics complained bitterly about proselytism and the lack of freedom in controlling their own education. In his pastoral of January 21, 1867, for the feast of St. Brigid, Cardinal Cullen criticized Dr. Whately, the Archbishop of Canterbury, for "supporting national education with the view of undermining our religion, of supplanting what he calls the vast fabric of the Irish Roman Catholic Church."[35] Herein, therefore, lies one of the basic reasons for Catholic agitation for disestablishment. As long as the Establishment remained, the national education effort seemed in the eyes of Catholics, only a threat to the survival of their own religion. They bitterly resented the imposition of Protestantism upon them against their will through religious educational means.

---

[33] Freeman's Journal, July 4, 1871.

[34] "The Education Question in Ireland," Saturday Review, XXVIII (September, 1869), p. 341.

[35] Peader MacSuibhne, Paul Cullen and His Contemporaries (Kildare: Leinster Leader Ltd, 1965), III, p. 371.

On the eve of the formation of the National Association, James Kavanagh, a Roman Catholic who was appointed Superintendent of National Schools in 1845, had said that education would constitute an important part of the Association's program. The Association's main purpose was declared to be to seek reform in the landlord tenant relationship, the abolition of the Irish Church Establishment, and the perfect freedom of education in all its branches. Cardinal Cullen, who was very conscious of a lack of freedom in the existing system of education, pleaded that Government control of public schools should be limited to the right to provide funds for their maintenance, and that further State intervention should cease.

As in England, the Establishment in Ireland had insisted on the union of religious and secular instruction. On this, the Catholics disagreed, for they had always stressed the right of parents to educate their children in schools of their choice. On the whole, the Catholics looked upon the Establishment as a perpetual obstruction to their civil liberty. The removal of the Establishment, therefore, meant a whole deal to them in their struggle for freedom and equality of educational opportunity.

It is no wonder, then, that the Catholics renewed their claims for the denominational system immediately following disestablishment. This was evident by the end of 1869, when the Catholic bishops issued their Maynooth Resolutions demanding prompt attention to the university problem. At that time, too, the National Association leaders had been insisting that the Church settlement must be followed quickly by a settlement of the education question. The Times noted that the act which disestablished the Church had "affected a revolution which it is freely admitted necessarily involves some corresponding changes in the university system."[36] The Times also expressed the urgency of the university question in its remark that "the university question is rapidly coming to the front, and seems likely to take precedence of the land question in the order of legislation."[37] But Gladstone, contrary to the sequence suggested by the Times with the land problem next in the execution of his Irish policy.

Gladstone's policy of governing Ireland along Irish lines was given very careful consideration by the Catholic bishops.

---

[36] The Times, September 4, 1869, p. 7.

[37] Ibid., July 29, 1869.

Gladstone advocated that the Irish, while forming part of the United Kingdom, were a distinct people and should be treated as such. He was a firm believer in religious rights and liberty which he deemed to be among the beneficial results of disestablishment. This fact he clearly enunciated in a speech at Ormskirk on October 21, 1868:

> I cannot go as far as those who say it is neccessary to maintain an Established Church in order to secure the possession of religious liberty...The foundations of religious liberty are laid with perfect certainty and solidity on the principles of universal toleration and equality of religious rights.[38]

One year before, Gladstone, in a speech at Southport, had made it clear that "no man ought to be able to say that any one of these nations is governed according to the traditions, the views, or the ideas of another."[39] Consequently, Gladstone favored following a policy that was most suitable for the Irish.

The Catholic bishops did not hesitate to seize on this policy to their own advantage. In their September 1869 resolutions, they declared that they understood that it was the Government's intention "to legislate for Ireland in accordance with the wishes of its people," and therefore they wanted the Ministers of Government to know that it was their wish to have "a complete system of education based upon religion."[40] These tough demands followed in the wake of developments after disestablishment. GLadstone himself in his first election address in Southwest Lancashire in 1868, had said that "In removal of the Establishment I see the discharge of a debt of civil justice."[41]

---

[38]W. E. Gladstone, Speeches of the Right Hon. W. E. Gladstone M.P. delivered at Warrington, Ormskirk, Liverpool, Southport, Newton Leigh, and Wigan in October 1868 (London: Simpkin, Marshall & Co., 1868).

[39]J. L. Hammond, Gladstone and the Irish Nation (Hamden, Conn.: Archon Books, 1964), pp. 81-82.

[40]The Times, September 4, 1869, p. 7. Resolution IV.

[41]W. E. Gladstone, Speeches in Southwest Lancashire in October 1868 (Liverpool: Egerton Smith and Co., 1868), p. v.

All this gave great impetus to the bishops to press their claims for freedom, educational equality, and even a separate educational system. Monypenny and Buckle have correctly observed that "it is difficult not to connect the extremist attitude of the Irish negotiators with the development of Gladstone's policy of disestablishment."[42] The Irish Church Act itself wrought a great change at Maynooth which resulted in less State intrusion into the affairs of the college. Of this, John Healy wrote: "Henceforth it was released from all Government control. There could be no more Government Commissions, no more lay visitations, no more vexatious and calumnious debates in Parliament about the college, and that in itself was something of a gain."[43]

This severing of Maynooth College from the State as a result of disestablishment was in some respects heartening to the Irish bishops, who used the occasion to further their aims for separate denominational education. So imbued were they with this idea, that they were not even impressed with concurrent efforts to open up Trinity College. It is significant that Henry Fawcett, the radical member for Brighton, who made his first motion for the abolition of religious tests on June 18, 1867, renewed them at the time of the disestablishment of the Irish Church. His motions aimed at doing away with all religious tests at Trinity College, Dublin, and offering fellowships and foundation scholarships to persons who did not profess the religion of the Establishment.

As Fawcett introduced the Bill for the abolition of tests in 1869, he remarked that "the Prime Minister in his memorable speech introducing the Irish Church Bill had admitted that Trinity College must be dealt with."[44] It was fitting that such action, as Fawcett suggested, be taken at that time, although the motion did not succeed until 1873. The Establishment had fostered Protestant ascendancy in Ireland, in religious as well as educational matters and disestablishment would strike at the root of that ascendancy. Henry Fawcett's motion could therefore be considered an added weapon in the struggle to effect religious as well as educational equality, which the Catholics hoped for in disestablishment.

---

[42] W. F. Monypenny and G. E. Buckle, op.cit., II, p. 349.

[43] John Healy, *Maynooth College: Its Centenary History, 1795-1895* (Dublin, 1895), p. 480.

[44] Great Britain, 3 *Hansard's Parliamentary Debates*, 1869, CXCVIII, p. 1197.

But the Catholic bishops were not very happy with Fawcett's motion to abolish tests. In 1869, it was evident that they would not be satisfied with a mixed university. The Freeman's Journal, in July, 1861, voiced Catholic reaction to the proposals, which were gradually being countenanced by Trinity College officials.

> What means this sudden liberality on the part of Trinity College? How comes it that the self-same men who a few short years ago could scarce find terms strong enough to denounce the admission of Catholics and Dissenters to an equality with themselves are now so anxious to share with them the rich prizes and endowments of Old Trinity?[45]

This statement is indicative of Catholic distrust of Protestant moves to relax restrictions at Trinity College.

Moreover, in addition to Catholic distrust, there was something else; the Catholics were not really interested in the opening up of Trinity College. They feared that such a university would only repeat the evils of the Queen's Colleges at Belfast, Galway, and Cork which were created by Sir Robert Peel in 1845 to provide education for Catholics. By 1850, bitter denunciations of these institutions as godless colleges issued forth from the bishops who were very critical of the lack of provision for theological studies. The attempt to secularize Trinity College, therefore, did not appeal to the bishops in light of these circumstances. Furthermore, it was strongly agreed among Catholics that their faith and morals would be endangered by attendance at Trinity College even if religious tests were abolished. On these matters the Catholic laity, contrary to some expectations, firmly supported the bishops' educational demands in the Declaration of 1870.[46]

Religious problems had therefore complicated the settlement of the university question in Ireland. The solution depended not only upon the effect of disestablishment, but also upon the nature of Catholic objectives and claims. While the Liberals hoped to follow up disestablishment with a strengthening of the mixed

---

[45] Freeman's Journal, July 6, 1871.

[46] Great Britain, Parliamentary Papers, 1870, LIV, 645, "Copy of Declaration of Catholic Laity of Ireland, on the Subject of University Education...laid before the Prime Minister."

system, the Catholics looked forward more than ever to the denominational system which would give them full control over their education. There was no doubt about Catholic determination on this point.

In March, 1868, Archbishop Leahy of Cashel and Bishop Derry of Clonfert, presented a "Statement of the University Question" to the Catholic members of Parliament, pointing to the necessity of the endowment of the existing Catholic university rather than the creation of a new one by the State.[47] In his speech before Parliament in 1868, Gladstone also made reference to the Statement, which insisted that a bishop's right included not only the selecting and supervising of teachers, but also "examining, and if expedient, of rejecting books which it may be proposed to use in the University."[48] It was for this reason that Gladstone hesitated to implement the recommendations of the Powis Commission which was set up in 1868.

The Powis Commission made a two-year survey of education in Ireland, and in 1870, the report found that the National System of Education was denominational to a very large extent and should, as such, receive legal recognition. This report is one of the most important historical documents in Irish education. A portion of the report dealt with religion, and recommendations were made accordingly: Roman Catholic children should not be present when religious instruction was taught by Protestants and vice versa; children were not to be compelled to attend religious observances if their parents objected; religious emblems should not be exhibited during school hours.[49]

This emphasis on denominationalism could hardly be ignored, for the 1859 Commissioners' Report on National Education in Ireland had revealed the extent of mixed education in the National Schools for the last quarter of that year. It showed that in schools run entirely by Protestants only 3 1/2 per cent of Catholic children

---

[47]Great Britain, 3 Hansard's Parliamentary Debates, 1868, CXC, p. 1733.

[48]Ibid., p. 1753.

[49]Great Britain, Parliamentary Papers, 1870, XXVIII, Part I (Reports from Commissioners, Vol. XVII), c.b., May, 1870, Commission of Inquiry into Primary Education (Ireland), p. 526.

were given secular instruction as compared with 16 7/10 per cent of Protestant pupils under Catholic teachers.[50] The Powis Commission Report also emphasized religious equality in education, stating that where there was only one school in a district, instead of excluding all religious instruction, a general course should be adopted to accommodate all on an equal footing.

To the Catholics, educational equality was an expression of religious equality. In their Maynooth Resolutions of 1869, the bishops stated unequivocally their right to a Catholic University, although they admitted that religious equality had been met if "degrees, endowments, and other privileges enjoyed by their fellow students of a different religion be placed within the reach of Catholics."[51] Catholics had therefore welcomed the recommendations of the Powis Commission on religious education, for this was one way in which they conceived of educational equality. Other Catholics were not quite satisfied.

In 1872, the Freeman's Journal strongly stated that since as the result of disestablishment the Catholic religion had been placed on a level of perfect equality with all others, the claims of its adherents to denominational education "must therefore be examined on their intrinsic merits."[52] Anything savoring of inequality had long been frowned upon by the Catholics. At the annual meeting of the Catholic University in December, 1866, the very Rev. Monsignor Woodlock, Rector of the University, warned that "no arrangement can meet with the full approval of Catholics which does not place Catholic education on a perfect equality with every other system of education."[53]

But there was great concern among Protestants in England, as well as in Ireland, concerning the strong emphasis of the Catholics on equality. The dissatisfaction of some Catholics with the report of the Powis Commission which favored denominational education to some extent was not to be

---

[50] Great Britain, Parliamentary Papers, 1860, XXVI, Part I, "The Twenty-sixth Report o- the Commissioners of National Education in Ireland" (for the year 1859), p. xxix.

[51] Weekly Freeman's Journal, September 4, 1869, p. 4. (Resolution VI)

[52] Freeman's Journal, June 24, 1872.

[53] The Times, December 22, 1866.

taken lightly. It was felt that what the Catholics wanted was supremacy rather than more equality. Even before the Irish Church Act was passed many Protestants feared that disestablishment would encourage new leanings toward Ultramontanism on the part of Catholics. This concern was expressed in Professor J. S. Brewery's letter to The Times in April, 1868; and The Times concurred, stating that "we recognize with him the important bearing of the imminent change on religious liberty and sacerdotal assertions."[54] Yet there seemed to be some hope that after disestablishment there would be something in the constitutional atmosphere of the United Kingdom by which, as The Times remarked in September, 1869, "Liberalism could be reconciled with the pretensions of Ultramontanism."[55]

However, that delusion was quickly dispelled when on September 25, 1869, Cardinal Cullen issued a pastoral condemning the mixed system of education. Disestablishment had not long been settled. The Times remarked that the pastoral marked "the beginning of a new epoch of the educational controversy."[56] Even the Saturday Review commented that "as regards Cardinal Cullen's Pastoral, it is certainly difficult to find that common ground of which we are in search."[57] The pastoral seemed to spark new anti-Catholic feeling which became worse as the movement in Rome towards the definition of Papal Infallibility climaxed in 1870. By 1872, the Irish Catholic Union announced its main objectives, to promote the restoration of Papal supremacy throughout the world, and to oppose any interference with the authority of the Church and the parent in education.[58]

It was because of ultramontane designs that many Protestant leaders did not favor the disestablishment of the Irish Church. William Thompson, Archbishop of York, held the view in 1868 that the Irish Anglican Church was not necessarily established as the Church of the privileged or as a missionary Church for the conversion of Roman Catholics, but

---

[54]Ibid., April 10, 1868, p. 6.

[55]Ibid., September 4, 1869, p. 7.

[56]Ibid., September 3, 1869, p. 8.

[57]"The Education Question in Ireland", Saturday Review, XXVIII, 1869, p. 340.

[58]The Times, November 27, 1872, p. 5.

rather "as a living witness of the State against Popery."[59] In 1873, anti-Catholic sentiments were also voiced by the English Dissenters, who in opposition to Catholic demands for denominational education, declared that they were not prepared to allow "the Papist body to domineer in Ireland."[60] There is no question that the Catholics were united in their determination to have full sway over education in both school and college. The Catholic laity soon joined the clergy in demanding equality of educational opportunity for all Catholics.

In March, 1870, the declaration of the laity was a scathing attack on the existing system of education. They insisted that it was the constitutional right of all British subjects to choose their own form of collegiate or university education. The declaration ended with this demand:

> That we therefore demand such a change in the system of Collegiate and University education as will place those who entertain these conscientious objections on a footing of equality with the rest of their fellow countrymen as regards Colleges, University honours and emoluments, University Examinations, government and representation.[61]

Many Protestant leaders might have been taken by surprise by this declaration inasmuch as up to that time there was not too much cooperation between the clergy and the laity. It was well known that the Catholic bishops had everything in absolute control. Cardinal Manning did not foresee any threat to this, even if layment were to participate in the Government of the proposed university, as he wrote to Cardinal Cullen on February 20, 1868: "If they were to propose the admission of laymen into the Government, is it not possible to reserve the supreme control of the bishops over all this system?"[62]

---

[59]"The Irish Church," Saturday Review, XXVI 1868, p. 5.

[60]"Our State and Prospects," Blackwood's Magazine, CXIII February, 1873, p. 253.

[61]Great Britain, Parliamentary Papers, 1870, LIV 645, "Declaration of the Catholic Laity of Ireland on the Subject of University Education in that Country," p. 1.

[62]Dublin Review, Vol. 165, p. 182.

Accordingly, the wavering support of the laity for the bishops' university education demands changed with the prospect of disestablishment. In March, 1868, the laity issued a declaration in favor of disestablishment and "to contradict publicly the assertion that we do not feel aggrieved by the present ecclesiastical settlement of Ireland."[63]

Hence, one of the immediate effects of disestablishment was a unity of purpose among prelates and laity which was expressed in their efforts to secure denominational education. In September, 1870, the laity and the bishops issued a joint declaration demanding denominational education.[64] Consequently, Protestant attitude against Catholics became more hostile, the Liberals even refraining somewhat to communicate too much with the bishops because of the unfavorable state of public feeling. When, therefore, the Government decided not to reform Irish National Education along the lines suggested by the Powis Commission, it was to avoid giving the appearance of strengthening the bishops' hands. The bishops' hands had been already strengthened by disestablishment, however, and their determined actions were to show themselves in the bitter struggle over the university question in the 1870's.

---

[63]Great Britain, Parliamentary Papers, LIII, 75, "Declaration of the Roman Catholic Laity of Ireland."

[64]Weekly Freeman's Journal, September 24, 1870, p. 4.

CHAPTER III

THE LAND ISSUE

The Irish Catholic hierarchy became intensely interested in the land problem, for to a great extent any solution to the university question depended on the manner in which that problem was resolved. On August 14, 1869, the Weekly Freeman's Journal hinted at the great need for a settlement of the land question:

> Now that the great obstacle to the cooperation of Irishmen has been removed by the act which put an end to the Church Establishment, the first duty of all who love their country will be to take counsel together and devise a just settlement of the land question.[1]

It soon became quite clear, however, that the hierarchy's agitation for a solution to the land problem was inevitably linked to the university question. The Times stated in September, 1869, that "the education question keeps pace with the land question."[2] The education question like the Church and land questions, was concerned with property rights.

In January, 1869, Cardinal Cullen wrote to the National Association expressing confidence in Gladstone and Bright as they sought the passage of a measure to secure property rights.[3] Three months later Gladstone, speaking on the state of Ireland, admitted to Protestant ascendancy in land as well as Church:

> Nor can I admit that in dealing with the Church question, we are not in a sense dealing with the land for it has been the maintenance of Protestant ascendancy in the

___

[1] Weekly Freeman's Journal, August 14, 1869.

[2] The Times, September 4, 1869, p. 7.

[3] The Times, January 15, 1869, p. 4.

- 41 -

form of the religious Establishment, which
has been one great and paramount cause of the
mode in which the power of the landlord has
been used.[4]

In August, 1869, the Saturday Review noted that land was owned by the wrong persons. It objected to the existing ownership of land on three grounds: that the land owners were Protestants while most of the People in Ireland were Catholics; that the absentee practices of the landlords were hurting the tenants' cause; and that too much property was held by the landlords.[5] This Protestant ascendancy in land ownership greatly concerned the Gladstone Ministry.

The Irish Catholic hierarchy viewed Protestant ascendancy in land with even greater concern than it was viewed by the Gladstone Ministry. In their Maynooth resolutions of August, 1869, they admitted that they did recognize the rights and duties of the landlords; but in the same spirit they clamored for equal recognition of the rights and duties of tenants. At that time, too, the Weekly Freeman's Journal demanded "security to all classes by the legal protection of property, and the establishment of a land code on equal justice."[6] The Saturday Review expressed its support of these objectives in the following statement:

> As in the case of the Irish (Anglican) Church,
> Parliament confined itself to the definite, exceptional,
> remediable grievance of a state being imposed upon a
> community of nonconformists and endowed out of their
> property; so in the case of the Irish land, Parliament
> is invited to redress the definite, exceptional and
> remediable grievance that in Ireland the tenant is too
> much at the mercy of the owner of the land.

One of the biggest landowners in Ireland up to late in the nineteenth century was Trinity College. In 1904, a University Commission was appointed

---

[4] Great Britain, 3 Hansard's Parliamentary Debates, 1869, CXCV, pp. 2022-23.

[5] "The Irish Land Question," Saturday Review, XXVIII (October, 1869), p. 235.

[6] The Weekly Freeman's Journal, August 21, 1869, p. 4.

[7] "Irish Land," Saturday Review, Vol. XXVIII, 1869, p. 656.

to inquire into and report upon "the means by which the Purchase by the Occupying Tenants of their Holdings persuant to the provisions of the Land Purchase Acts may be facilitated without diminishing the average net rental derived by Trinity College as Head Landlord."[8] The Preamble to the Trinity College, Dublin, Leasing and Perpetuity Act of 1851, vested certain lands in the Provost of the College as such, and stated that it would be to the advantage of the College if the powers for making leases and grants were given to the Provost, Fellows, and Scholars. When it is remembered that these officials were Protestants, it is not difficult to understand the hardships borne by the tenants who were mainly Catholics. The Commissioner in 1904 noted that the Trinity College, Dublin, Leasing and Perpetuity Act, 1851, stated that "the tenants complained that the uncertainty of their tenure had prevented them from expending money in the improvement of land."[9]

The College lands consisted of valuable areas, demesnes, mills, villages, and even towns as well as other properties beyond the scope of the Land Law Acts. Enormous sums (about Ł30,000) were collected in rents from the several estates in the nineteenth century. These estates extended over the whole country; according to the Right Hon. Gerald Fitz-Gibbon, Chairman of the Trinity College, Dublin, Estates Commission, in 1904, "the College estates are curiously distributed over Ireland."[10] Many Protestant landlords in various parts of Ireland were rent-payers to the College. Mr. Horner, K.C., who gave evidence before the 1904 Commission referred to the Earl of Leitrim in the County of Donegal as one of these.[11] His estate included some 30,000 acres occupied by 872 tenants. Rent increase on many estates was a regular feature and this made it difficult for tenants. Mr. Horner noted that a certain lease on the Leitrim estates had increased from Ł1,932 19^s in 1849, to Ł2,555 8^s 4^d in 1853, and to Ł3,072 12^s 3^d in 1863.

As Head Landlord, Trinity College was entitled to at least 50 percent of what was collected from the various estates. In his evidence to the Commission, Mr. Matheson, K.C., reported that out of the total rents of Ł4,088 16^s 10^d received from the occupying tenants on

---

[8] Great Britain, *Parliamentary Papers*, 1905, XXVII, "Report of Trinity College, Dublin, Estates Commission," p. 1.

[9] *Ibid.*, p. 17.

[10] *Ibid.*, Appendix of Evidence, p. 2.

[11] *Ibid.*, p. 16.

Mr. Kirk's estate in Armagh, ₤2,441 13^s 6^d was paid to the College.[12] The College had great economic power; it could deny certain renewals or it could require an increased rent of due proportion to the value of land.

Compared with Trinity College, the Catholic College at Maynooth did not have nearly as much land. This seminary, picturesquely situated a few miles from Dublin in the County of Kildare, occupied the former property of the Duke of Leinster. The whole of the Leinster estate consisted of 67,000 acres, Maynooth College occupying only a small portion of this. Trinity College, on the other hand, possessed extensive land all over Ireland numbering almost one-hundred estates. The site on which Trinity College was erected was confiscated from a monastery, and from the start it was endowed with large tracts of land also confiscated from the Irish Catholics.

Confiscations by force were quite common in the reigns of Cromwell, Charles II, and William III. The ultimate result of the Cromwellian conquest was to establish in Ireland three or four thousand landowners of English blood and Puritan leanings in the midst of a vanquished population. Charles II confirmed the Cromwellian forfeitures. The Catholic James II was superceded in 1689 by the Protestant William III in whose reign confiscations were renewed and brought to a climax. Protestant ascendancy thus continued in landownership as in Church and State affairs in Ireland as well as in England.

This Protestant ascendancy was reflected in the property arrangements of Trinity College and Maynooth College; for this reason, developments in higher education were bound to be effected by the resultant economic situation. The total revenue from all sources of Trinity College, including her rents from chambers, and contingent receipts from the year 1869 amounted to ₤59,932 6^s 4^d.[13] The State endowment of Maynooth was less than one quarter of the Crown lands of Trinity College, which valued some ₤30,000 per annum. While Trinity College was either direct or head landlord of over 200,000 acres of land, Maynooth College stood in no such position. It is true that in 1868 Maynooth received the sum of ₤26,251 10^s 11^d from the Consolidate Fund.[14] This amount, however, could hardly meet the full

_____

[12]Ibid., p. 15.

[13]Parliamentary Papers, 1874, LI, 701, "Return of the Total Revenue from All Sources of Trinity College, Dublin, for each year from 1869 to 1873," p. 2.

[14]Great Britain, Parliamentary Papers, 1867-68, LIII, 805, "Return of Amount received by the Royal College of St. Patrick Maynooth from the Consolidated Fund in each year since 1840," p. 6.

expense of that college. The Commissioners appointed to visit Maynooth in 1864 pointed out that the total unexpended surplus of the funds, that is, the balance of the Dunboyne Estate, to the exclusive benefit of which students were entitled, "only amounted at the end of the last financial year to the sum of £16 13^s 6^d."[15]

Due to lack of adequate funds, the physical condition of Maynooth College was far from desirable. In their report, the visiting Commissioners of 1864 expressed shock at what they saw at the college:

> We were struck by the crowded condition of the Hall in which the students were assembled for the visitation and still more on visiting the chapel by the manifest inadequacies of the latter to the accommodation of so numerous a community, as well as by the poverty of the fittings and its inappropriateness for the services of a collegiate body...We learned with regret from the report of the President that the Trustees have been constrained to make some retrenchments in the dietary of the students.[16]

The situation at Maynooth was very bad. In 1860, Dr. C. W. Russell, the President of Maynooth, told the visiting Commissioners, "I regret, however, to be obliged to direct the attention of the Visitors to a number of glaring and most painful deficiencies which still remain... even with the addition of new buildings."[17] The president made reference to poor ventilation, inadequate library space, lack of furniture, insufficient lighting, and other needs. He also pointed to the lack of a hall large enough to accommodate the entire college community for academic exhibitions, distribution of prizes, or for any other public exercises.

The accommodation at Trinity College, on the other hand, was quite adequate. Indeed, the enormous wealth of this Protestant institution made pos-

---

[15]Great Britain, <u>Parliamentary Papers</u>, 1865, XLIII, 451, "Report of the Visitors of Maynooth College, 1864," p. 1.

[16]Great Britain, <u>Parliamentary Papers</u>, XLIII, 1865, 451, "Report of the Visitors of Maynooth, 1864," p. 4.

[17]<u>Ibid</u>., 1860, LIII, 655, "Report of a Visitation held at Maynooth College on the 20 day of June 1860," p. 5.

sible the acquisition of the most impressive facilities. Griffith's evaluation of the gross rental of Crown lands amounted to ₤70,907 $7^s_{\ 18}$, and rentals from privately donated lands was ₤11,242 9^s in 1867. Trinity College could thus afford to provide the best accommodation for its 1392 students, only 76 of which were Catholics.[19] At Maynooth there were 534 students in 1864.[20] Hence Catholics were at a great disadvantage at both institutions. A mere handful of their number enjoyed the privileges at Trinity College, while at their own institution the situation was not at all good.

At Maynooth there was neither land nor money to spare. In 1867, ₤6,965 $7^s\ 9^d$ was voted for repair and maintenance at that college, but ₤6,988 $2^s\ 4^d$ was expended.[21] Trinity College had plenty of land and was consequently wealthy, while the need for more land at Maynooth continued to be sharply felt. In 1860, the Trustees of Maynooth observed that the Commissioners of Public Works had been constituted commissioners for the purposes of "enlarging, improving, upholding, and maintaining, repairing, fitting up, and furnishing from time to time the buildings and premises connected with the college."[22] It should be noted that enlargement of the premises was given first consideration.

In order to enlarge the premises and improve the buildings, more money was needed. In their memorial to the Lord Lieutenant in 1860, the Trustees of Maynooth College made special reference to the fact that a request by the Commissioners of Public Works in 1845 for additional funds for Maynooth "encountered in Parliament the opposition of the same party which had resisted the substantive measure of endowment."[23] The Trustees further

---

[18] Great Britain, Parliamentary Papers, 1867-68, LIII, 805, "Returns Relative the Revenues of Trinity College and Maynooth College," p. 2.

[19] Ibid., p. 3.

[20] Ibid., XLIII, 1865, 451, "Report of the Visitors of Maynooth College, 1864." p. 2.

[21] Ibid., LIII, 1867-68, 805, "Returns Relative to the Revenues of Trinity College and Maynooth College," p. 5.

[22] Ibid., 1860, LIII, 655, "Copies of a Memorial addressed by the Trustees of the Royal College of Saint Patrick, Maynooth, to the Lord Lieutenant of Ireland, with respect to the Repairs of the College," p. 1.

[23] Ibid.

pointed out that in 1852, the item of "Repairs of Maynooth College" was altogether omitted from the Estimates; and "at length," the memorial continued, "during the religious excitement which prevailed in the following year, on the votes being re-proposed, it was struck out of the Estimates by a small majority of the Committee."[24]

Such omissions must have been very discouraging to the Catholics. They had been experiencing religious and civil inequality, which had adversely affected their educational aspirations. The problems were further aggravated by inequality in land distribution which was directly or indirectly impeding their goals for higher education. The 1860 memorial report was signed by Cardinal Cullen, Archbishop Joseph Dixon of Armagh, Archbishop John MacHale of Tuam, Archbishop Patrick Leahy of Cashel, and others. These men, no doubt, were quite familiar with the inequities in the distribution of land in Ireland.

The land questions continued to be a problem for Maynooth. According to the Bursar of the College, in 1867 "the only land from which the (Maynooth) College receives any rent is the Dunboyne Estate, containing 438 acres...let under fee-farm grant at the gross annual rent of £461 18^s 2^d."[25] In addition, the Royal College of St. Patrick, Maynooth, was erected on land held in perpetuity containing 123 acres for which the college paid £194 10^s 6^d per annum. As tenant at will, the college also held a farm from his Grace, the Duke of Leinster, consisting of 218 acres at a rental of £300 per annum.[26]

Hence while Trinity College was a great landlord, Maynooth College was but a tenant. The Roman Catholic prelates have hardly ever complained of the inequality in higher education without reference to the vast areas of land held by Trinity College. In their Memorial to Sir George Grey, Secretary of State for Home Affairs, 1866, the prelates stated that the landed property of Trinity College or the University of Dublin was equal to "100th part of the hole acreage of Ireland."[27] The prelates referred to the large pecuniary resources enjoyed by that college.

---

[24]Ibid.

[25]Great Britain, Parliamentary Papers, 1867-68, LIII, 805, "Returns Relative to the Revenues of Trinity College and Maynooth College," p. 6.

[26]Ibid.

[27]Great Britain, Parliamentary Papers, 1866, LV, 243, "Copies of Memorials addressed to the Secretary of State for the Home Department on the Subject of National and University Education in Ireland," p. 6.

The Catholic prelates continued to emphasize the advantages of the landed wealth of Trinity College or Dublin University and the way it had benefited Protestant higher education:

> The advantages enjoyed by the Protestant University of Dublin do not stop here: schools connected with it are scattered throughout Ireland, and possess extensive property in lands, granted in part by the Crown, the Royal Schools, Endowed Schools, and Erasmus Smith's Schools. They may be considered as intended exclusively for the benefit of members of the Established Church, although a few boys of other religious denominations are occasionally admitted; and they serve very largely as feeders of the Protestant University.[28]

Noting that "the income and influence derived from such extensive landed property must be considerable," the prelates stated that "the advantages offered by an institution so richly endowed have always attracted great numbers to its lecture halls."[29]

The Irish Catholic prelates continued to press for a Charter for the Catholic University which they had established in an attempt to meet their needs. They had collected ₤125,000 in a few years for the foundation and maintenance of the Catholic University, and had "purchased premises in the City of Dublin, gathered together a library of about 30,000 volumes, scientific collections, and appointed a body of professors of great eminence."[30] The prelates complained that they were "cramped, however, in many ways," and pleaded that "in order to place this new Catholic College on a footing of equality with other institutions, a suitable endowment be given to it."[31]

Never did the cry for religious and educational equality cease. In 1879, the Roman Catholic Laity of Ireland reiterated the opinions expressed by their fellows in 1869, that "perfect religious equality involves equality

---

[28] Ibid.

[29] Ibid.

[30] Ibid., p. 8.

[31] Ibid., p. 10.

in all educational advantages afforded by the State."[32] Certainly, one way of doing this would be through an equal distribution of land which would provide the financial means to better educational opportunities, for indeed, the quality of education can hardly be divorced from its financing. Much depends on the resources available and the effective use made of them, if education must meet the aspirations of the people. Archbishop Cullen and the other bishops who agitated for educational equality knew this very well. They were fully aware of the facts of the land situation and the way it was affecting education. As the Times remarked in July, 1869, the Establishment had precluded them not only from control of the Trinity College curriculum, but also from "a share in the financial administration."[33]

Bewildered by all of these educational problems, it was no wonder, then, that the Catholics pressed for land legislation. After all, there were more Catholics in Ireland than there were Protestants, and yet the great bulk of the landed property was in the hands of Protestants, many of whom were absentee landlords. During the latter part of 1869, several meetings, many of them attended by priests of the Deanery of Dunmore, headed by Patrick Duffy, assembled in Conference to consider demands for future land legislation in Ireland. The demands included State purchase of the property of absentee landlords and resale to the occupiers.[34] Soon a common spirit animated both clergy and laity as they concentrated their efforts on the land question.

The land question presented great difficulty to the Catholic hierarchy. The emphasis placed on this question at the end of their 1869 Maynooth Resolutions clearly revealed their sense of the difficulty. The resolutions reflected a great deal of concern for the education question, and their appeal for immediate consideration of the land question was an expression of their undying consciousness of the importance of that question to education. The Freeman's Journal captured the bishops mood:

> Therefore, in the interests of all classes, they earnestly hope that the responsible advisers of the Crown will take this most important

---

[32]Great Britain, **Parliamentary Papers**, 1878-79, LVII, 495, "Copy of Declaration of Catholic Laity of Ireland, on the subject of University Education in that country," p. 1.

[33]The Times, July 29, 1869, p. 10.

[34]Weekly Freeman's Journal, October 9, 1869, p. 4.

subject into consideration, and propose to
Parliament such measures as may restore
confidence, stimulate industry, increase
national wealth, and lead to general union,
contentment and happiness.[35]

The bishops desired a system of education, "founded on a basis of freedom and of religious and financial equality,"[36] as Thomas Pope so clearly stated. It is evident that the bishops were very mindful of the economic aspects of the situation which depended so much on land. They wished for new land legislation which would not only alter the balance in higher education, but also improve the general welfare of the people. the Government was expected to do something about the land problem, just as it had successfully carried through disestablishment.

Soon after disestablishment, Gladstone became even more aware of the need for land legislation. The disendowment aspects of the Irish Church Act of 1869 had touched the land problem. One of the main objectives of that Act was to bring about a more equal distribution of Church lands, by breaking down the immense possessions of the Irish Anglican Establishment and by building up the property of the lesser churches. Widespread dissatisfaction had followed severe attacks, not only on the vast landed estates of the absentee landlords, but also on those of the Anglican Church.

A great many of the landowners were themselves Anglican Protestants. In 1869, the Saturday Review observed that "it was the theory that the ownership of land is in the hands of the wrong people that provoked Mr. Gladstone to denounce in the present position of Irish proprietorship one of the pestilential effects of the Upas Tree of Protestant ascendancy."[37] For three months after the passage of the Irish Church Act, Gladstone concentrated on the land problem, and on October 31, 1869, his cabinet met to discuss the Irish Land Bill. Gladstone then introduced its first reading on February

---

[35] Weekly Freeman's Journal, September 4, 1869, p. 4.

[36] Thomas Pope, The Council of the Vatican and the Events of the Time (Boston: Patrick Donahoe, 1872), p. 223.

[37] "The Irish Land Question," Saturday Review, XXVIII, 1869, p. 235.

15, 1870. The bill passed its second reading in the House of Lords and became law as it received the Royal Assent on August 1, 1870.[38]

By the Land Act of 1870, Gladstone legalized the Ulster Tenant Right for the whole of Ireland. The Ulster custom secured compensation for improvements, which was somewhat of a safeguard against wanton eviction. The Act did not officially make the tenant a co-owner of the land, although it proceeded by indirect methods to assure him the advantage which flowed from a tacit recognition of partnership in land. Under certain conditions it granted the right of compensation: first, for disturbance in case of arbitrary eviction, and second, for improvements by the tenant. In its original form, the clause dealing with this, stated that where "a tenant is disturbed in his holding by the act of the landlord,... the tenant so disturbed shall be entitled to such compensation as the Court may find to be payable to him according to the usage to which the holding is proved to be subject."[39]

But the Lords objected to the clause, and the Commons, in an attempt at compromise, confined it to a £15 rent limit. This did not please the Catholic bishops who had exerted great pressure for including in the bill the principles of perpetuity of tenure and judicially fixed rent. They had aimed at co-ownership of land, and felt the disappointment keenly. The bishops expressed to Gladstone, through Cardinal Manning, their dissatisfaction that the bill could not be regarded as a settlement of the question.

The Catholic bishops continued to demand equality. Early in 1869, the bishops' views on Church, land, and education questions were aired as their letters were read at a meeting of the National Association. Cardinal Cullen's letter emphasized that "the Catholics of this country cannot rest satisfied till they are placed on a

---

[38] Annual Register, 1870, p. 49.

[39] Great Britain, Parliamentary Papers, Vol. II (Bill, No. 29), February, 1870, "A Bill to Amend the Law relating to the Occupation and Ownership of Land in Ireland," pp. 1-2.

footing of perfect equality with their Protestant fellow subject."[40] Dr. William Keane, Bishop of Cloyne, speaking for the Irish people, stated that "equality is their birthright--equality their demand. On this cardinal point, no compromise, no shuffling, can be tolerated."[41] This equality, Dr. Michael O'Hea, Bishop of Poss, pointed out "can never be secured but by the disestablishment and total disendowment of the Church as by law established in Ireland."[42] His letter went on at great length to advocate a land bill and a measure of "free education" in Ireland. The Chairman of the National Association, Peter Paul MacSweeney, alarmed at cries for substantial re-endowment of the Irish Church from Protestant leaders expressed the fact that the people demanded and expected "complete disestablishment through disendowment."[43]

MacSweeney was quite emphatic in his condemnation of the confiscation of Catholic lands, suggesting that even the first Reformation endowments of the Irish Church should not be left. Accordingly, he put forward the following argument:

> If the Government seized the old Catholic glebe, effaced the old boundary, and set up a new glebe on the other side of the hedge, it is clear that such new glebe was or ought to be, nothing more or less than compensation to the people for their old glebe...taken from them, and therefore that it falls into the general mass of Church property, of which we have been defrauded for 300 years, and of which we now demand restitution.[44]

Notwithstanding their firm demands, the Catholic leaders gave their support to Gladstone and Bright on the land question for the time being, at least. Their emphasis on disendowment showed their

---

[40] The Times, January 15, 1869, p. 5.

[41] Ibid.

[42] Ibid.

[43] Ibid.

[44] Ibid.

concern for the landed property of the Irish Church. The wealth of the
Protestant Church due to its lands was also expressed in the wealth
and progress of Trinity College, which stood in stricking contrast to the
poor condition of Maynooth College or the Catholic University.
It will be remembered that many Catholic leaders who were members
of the Board of Trustees of Maynooth, had complained bitterly of the
financial situation of Maynooth which was traceable in part to its
lack of landed property and adequate endowment. The Liberals were
surely mindful of all this as they considered the glebes question.
They were concerned that if the houses and glebes of the clergy of
the Irish Church, when disestablished, were not to be taken from
them, then the other denominations should not be left in an unequal
position.

On January 18, 1869, H. A. Bruce, who made informal representations
to the Irish bishops of the Mayo plan for a Catholic University, spoke
to the land question at Lochwinnoch in Renfrewshire. He was asked
whether he would vote for the abolition of the Maynooth grant. His
reply expressed how closely allied were the land and university questions with the Church question in Ireland. Bruce declared that it
was left for the Government to decide whether to refuse to leave the
houses and glebes in the possession of the Protestant clergy or to so
compensate Maynooth as to put Catholics in a position of perfect equality.[45] A few days later Gladstone's reference to the same problem confirmed the close relationship between the land and university question,
both of which were being affected by the policy of disestablishment.
Writing to Fortescue on January 30, 1869, concerning the Maynooth clauses
to be inserted in the Irish Church Bill, Gladstone explained that the Maynooth compensation was considered in association with Protestant glebes.[46]

Gladstone, too, was well aware that if the Church lands were returned
to Protestant hands without due compensation to the Catholics, even greater
dissatisfaction might be aroused. In 1868, John Bright had admitted that
if the glebes were to be retained by Protestants, then the Catholics should
be entitled to a corresponding fixed property. Bright was also in favor
of land purchase which appealed to the Catholics. While the Catholics
frowned on concurrent endowment and would not accept any gifts of glebes
or glebe-houses, they wished to have more land by purchase. On the whole,

---

[45]Ibid., January 20, 1869, p. 3.

[46]Carlingford Papers, CP 1/26 Gladstone to Fortescue, January 30,
1869, as referred to be E. R. Norman, The Catholic Church and Ireland
in the Age of Rebellion, 1859-1873, p. 372.

the Catholic hierarchy fell in line with the considerations of the National Association, embracing the two broad plans of land purchase and fixity of tenure.

In January, 1869, Archbishop Leahy of Cashel sent a memorial from his flock to Gladstone seeking the possession through purchase, of an old church which belonged to the Establishment. This was a site, as Leahy wrote to Gladstone, "dear to all Ireland for its historical recollections."[47] The Catholic bishops followed this up with other plans for acquiring old Catholic sites by purchase. Gladstone viewed these plans with great concern, and wrote to Queen Victoria on the apparent danger of being too generous to the Protestant Church:

> To give to the disestablished Church the small portion of property conferred by the State since the Reformation, might give colour to a dangerous claim on the part of the R. C. Church to be reinstated in possession of the property presented to it by the State before the Reformation, and from this claim it might be difficult, on principle of equal dealing, to escape.[48]

In order to reinforce this principle of equality, Gladstone decided to push ahead with the Glebe Loans Bill as a supplement to the Irish Church Act. Inadvertently, the Irish Church Act had already touched upon the land problem by the special provision for the sales of any residue of Church estates by the Church Commissioners. The Irish Church Act was also the first to provide State aid for land purchase, and the Glebe Loans Bill was to expand on this. For this, Gladstone received the full backing of the Irish Catholic hierarchy.

On August 3, 1870, the Glebe Loans Bill passed its third reading in the House of Commons with a majority of twenty-two votes.[49] It also passed the House of Lords and became law on August 10, 1870. The Bill gave authority to the Commissioners of Public Works (Ireland) to loan as much as three-fourths

---

[47] Gladstone Papers, B.M. Add. MS. 44418, f. 232, Leahy to Gladstone, January 30, 1869, as quoted by E. R. Norman, op.cit., p. 361

[48] George Buckle (ed.), The Letters of Queen Victoria, 1862-1885, Vol. I. p. 581, Gladstone to the Queen, February 1, 1869.

[49] Great Britain, 3 Hansard's Parliamentary Debates, CCIII (1870), p. 1486.

of the amount needed for glebe purchases.[50] The Bill held substantial benefits not only for the Catholics who initially refused to accept any share of the disendowed property of the Irish Anglican Church, but also the Presbyterians. John Maguire, representative for the city of Cork, extolled the Bill as helping to bring about visible religious equality. In 1871, the Glebe Loans Bill was amended by a statute which provided for additional loans for other purposes.

These additional loans were of tremendous significance for the Irish Catholics. One of the other purposes to which they needed to apply additional loans for lands was that of higher education. As far as the Catholics were concerned, equality in educational opportunity was still far from being realized for them. The situation had little improved from what it was in 1841 when Thomas Wyse, Member of Parliament, wrote to the Right Honourable Lord Viscount Morpeth, then Chief Secretary for Ireland, pleading for the establishment of provincial colleges in Ireland. It is true that the Queen's Colleges were established in 1845, but the Catholics were in no way satisfied with them.

In his letter to Lord Morpeth, Thomas Wyse stated: "It is a grievance unheard of, I believe, in any country in Europe, that for a population of 8,000,000, one university only should be provided," and from which "seven-eigths of that population should be peremptorily excluded."[51] Wyse spoke highly of the intellectual side of college life, but also noted that "financial considerations are, of course, not to be excluded." He further elaborated on the financial aspects:

> From estimates furnished it is calculated that from 15,000 to 20,000 pounds would be sufficient with due economy, to defray the establishing of a moderately-sized provincial

---

[50]Great Britain, Parliamentary Papers, Vol. II (Bill 222), July, 1870, "A Bill to Amend the Act of the first and second years of His Late Majesty, King William the fourth, chapter thirty-three in part, and to afford facilities for the erection, enlargment and improvement of Glebe Houses, and for the acquirements of Lands for Glebes in Ireland," p. 2.

[51]Great Britain, Parliamentary Papers, 1867-68, LIII, 765, "Copy of a letter addressed officially to the Right Honourable Lord Viscount Morpeth, Late Chief Secretary for Ireland, by Thomas Wyse, Esq., M.P., on the 8th Day of May, 1841, relative to the Establishment and Support of Provincial Colleges in Ireland," p. 2.

college in the south of Ireland, comprising
under that head, purchase of a small quantity
of land, the erection of plain substantial
buildings, an outfit on a limited scale
sufficient for a commencement.[52]

Thomas Wyse's statement was tantamount to a direct appeal for more land for the buildings of colleges whereby Catholics could have better educational opportunities. Twenty years later, the Irish bishops approached the situation in a more indirect way. They had shown great interest in the disendowment aspects of the disestablished Church, which involved the land problem. They gave strong support to the Glebe Loans Bill which was a supplement to the Irish Church Act. All this was to affect a gradual transfer of land ownership from Protestant to Catholic hands. No doubt, it was for this reason that the Catholics were so anxious for a settlement of the land question.

Further evidence of Catholic interest in a quick settlement of the land question was revealed in an address by Peter MacSweeney before the National Association on July 27, 1869:

> Disestablishment is complete. Well, that alone is an enormous gain, and although Disendowment is not so fully carried out as the Bill originally contemplated...if the speedy carriage of the Church Bill hastened a settlement of the Land Question, I maintain that that consideration alone was worth far more than the few thousand pounds borne off as booty...by the Disestablished and Disendowed party.[53]

MacSweeney very adroitly revealed the great importance attached to land ownership. It was not merely the question of money to be considered here, but indeed the question of influence as well, for land ownership carries with it a great deal of influence.

If then the Irish bishops could upset the system of land ownership, and swing it more in their favor, their influence would be increased and this they could use to achieve their educational objectives. Supremacy and aristocracy accompanied Protestant ownership of land, and the result

---

[52] Ibid., p. 6.

[53] *Weekly Freeman's Journal*, July 31, 1869, p. 3.

was a superior education for Protestants. Break up the present system of land ownership, and this ill-balance in education would be overturned. The bishops, who were fully aware of the adverse effect of unequal land ownership on higher education, were determined to see the system changed; and it was for this reason mainly, that they continued to lend their support to the Land Bill of 1870, which they regarded as a hopeful sign.

Catholic support of the Land Bill of 1870 was further expressed when Cardinal Manning sent Gladstone a copy of the Irish bishops' memorandum for amendments to the proposed Land Bill, outlining the principles of perpetuity of tenure, and the adjustment of rent by a "Land Court." These two principles were important for, as J. L. Hammond noted, they were included in the provisions that became law in 1881.[54] The most important provisions of that Act were those reforming the existing system of land tenure. The Three F's Act--Fair Rent, Fixity of Tenure, and Free sale--were granted.[55] A Judicial Tribunal was also established by which Fair Rent and Fixity of Tenure were secured.

The Land Acts of 1870 and 1881 had far-reaching implications for higher education. J. L. Hammond has also stated that "the Act of 1870 had checked the process, which by treating Ireland as if she were an English county, has brought her agriculture and her people to ruin," while "the Act of 1881 was a turning point in her history."[56] The latter had an immediate effect in stimulating a policy of land purchase. Indeed, it created the conditions under which land purchase became possible on an extensive scale, and that made it possible for the Catholic Church to increase its acreage and build up its educational institutions.

In general, the provisions for land reform somewhat aided the Ultramontane designs of the Catholics. The transfer of land ownership which resulted in the gradual withdrawal of Protestant magnates and gentry in many areas, made it easier for Catholic supremacy to assert itself. commenting on the effect of land purchase, Michael J. McCarthy has observed that there was bound to be a "loss of Protestant professional men as well as of Protestant gentry," and that "the new professional men

---

[54]J. L. Hammond, Gladstone and the Irish Nation (London: Longmans Green and Co., 1938), p. 103.

[55]Great Britain, Parliamentary Papers, 1881, III, "Irish Land Law 1881," pp. 1-35.

[56]J. L. Hammond, Gladstone and the Irish Nation, p. 226.

will be educated by the (Catholic) Church." McCarthy stated further that "the hierarchy will gradually occupy the place of the nobility, and the priesthood that of the landed gentry."[57]

McCarthy also emphasized the effectiveness of the influence of the Catholic priesthood in the educational struggle: "Whenever the Irish are organized by their priests, "they will always be found fighting against the State system of education, and insisting on getting Government grants for exclusive Roman Catholic schools."[58] A few leading Protestants who were prominent in the land struggle had joined the Nationalists and the Catholic Church in advancing the Catholic educational program. Men like Sir John Gray, Isaac Butt, William Shaw, Thomas Dairs, and Charles Steward Parnell were strong advocates of just land legislation.

In 1869, Lord Bessborough was rebuked in London for encouraging Gladstone to seek the cooperation of Sir John Gray, Protestant proprietor of the Freeman's Journal, in the land legislation. The Irish Lord Chancellor, Lord Thomas O'Hagan, was then quick to reply that "the success or failure of the Land Bill depends on the Freeman's Journal; if it says, we accept this as a fixity of tenure, every priest will say the same, and vice versa."[59] Isaac Butt, the great Home Rule leader, was also involved in the land problem. Butt's definition of fair rent was that which a solvent and responsible tenant could afford to pay, and his program of Home Rule for Ireland was welcomed by many Catholic leaders, among them John MacHale, Archbishop of Tuam.

In May, 1871, John MacHale published an open letter to Gladstone in which he discussed the demand for religious education as the prime motive for Home Rule:

> Many...look for home government as a means to obtain the blessings of a Catholic education... The longer educational justice is denied us the louder and more pressing will be the demand for our own Parliament, since there are none...who are not convinced that had we our own legislature,

---

[57] M. J. McCarthy, *Irish Land and Irish Liberty* (London: Robert Scott, 1911), p. 378.

[58] Ibid., p. 381.

[59] John Morley, *The Life of William Ewart Gladstone*, Vol. II, p. 292.

it is not one university that would satisfy our
just demands, but like Scotland and England, too,
should have an adequate number of universities.[60]

Like the university reform movement, the Home Rule movement was influenced by developments in the land legislation. Indeed, it was the failure of the Land Act of 1870 to satisfy the demands of the tenant leaders which gave Isaac Butt his opportunity to launch the agitation for self-government. Tenants had discovered that while the Bill sought to give them protection from the worst kinds of eviction, it had not secured to them fixity of tenure and fair rents. They saw the possibility of evasion of the Bill's provisons by some landlords who could simply raise rent. The tenants viewed this unpleasant situation with alarm and much dissatisfaction.

Tenant dissatisfaction was quickly exploited by the clergy in an attempt to achieve their education demands. It is true that Cardinal Cullen, although he had a deep feeling for the poor, had tried to suppress the Tenant League priests for fear that they would become involved in violent activities. But it was difficult to keep the priests from involvement with the tenants, for the priests had sprung from the people. Indeed, Cullen himself was the son of a Carlow tenant farmer, and many of the other archbishops, bishops, and other dignitaries were sons of the common people. This close affinity between the Catholic priesthood and the people was of mutual advantage. The tenants looked to the clergy for support in the land problem, and the clergy mobilized them in return as they pressed for educational considerations.

In October, 1869, the Saturday Review observed that the priests were "mixing themselves up in the Land Question:"

> They have raised fixity of tenure into a sort of religious cry, and they avow the principle that everything is to be got that can be got out of England, and that it is to be got in any way. The Education Question is being tacked on to the Land Question.[61]

The Saturday Review further pointed to the tactics in manipulating the tenantry for educational ends:

---

[60] Weekly Freeman's Journal, May 13, 1871, p. 8.

[61] "The Irish Land Question," Saturday Review, XXVIII, Ocotber, 1869, p. 527.

> The priests seem to be driving a tacit
> bargin with the tenantry, and to be offering
> to support them in the most extreme demands
> for changes in the holding of land, provided
> that the tenants in their turn will support
> their priests in destroying every scheme of
> education in Ireland which is not absolutely
> under priestly control.[62]

The implications of this mutuality between the priesthood and the tenantry are by no means slight when it is considered that the struggle for Catholic control of university education has been somewhat synchronous with that for Catholic ownership of land. While the events of the decade under review (1869-1879) were only a prelude to their fulfillment, they have indeed, been very significant. Land purchase was first facilitated by the provisions of the Glebe Loans Act in 1870 following disestablishment when holdings could be bought from the Church Commissioners. The Bright Clauses of the 1870 Irish Land Act further encouraged land purchase as did the Land Act of 1881. The policy of land purchase with State aid was a positive feature from 1885, and by the end of the nineteenth century a great many Catholic tenants had become landowners. In 1909, Mr. Birrell, the Chief Secretary for Ireland, stated in the House of Commons that "previous to the Act of 1903 the sum of ₤24,000 had been advanced for land purchase, and 2½ millions of acres of land had been disposed of under the operations of the various Land Acts."[63] In this way, thousands of acres of land passed into Catholic ownership.

This impressive increase in Catholic ownership of land was simultaneous with the establishment of the new National University in Dublin in 1908 to meet the demands of the Catholic hierarchy. "The persistence with which the hierarchy pursued their agitation for a Catholic University, first in the peaceful years before 1879, and afterwards through all the turmoil of the Land Agitation," wrote Michael J. MacCarthy, "well illustrates the peculiar ability of the clergymen of the Church of Rome."[64]

It was highly advantageous for the Catholic clergymen to involve themselves in the land issue as a means to promote their higher education objectives. Protestant ascendancy was clearly evident in land, as it was

---

[62] Ibid.

[63] Great Britain, 3 Hansard's Parliamentary Debates, 1909, III, p. 189.

[64] M. J. McCarthy, op.cit., p. 34.

in university education. It follows, therefore, that a reduction of
Protestant ascendancy in land ownership would produce a similar effect
in higher education. This was the main objective to which the efforts
of the Irish hierarchy were directed in their support of a peasant proprietary. The bishops strongly declared for land purchase, tenant right,
compensation for improvements, and fixity of tenure, which are indeed
the ingredients of a peasant proprietary.

Bearing in mind the priests' determination in matters relating to
a peasant proprietary, Cardinal Manning warned Gladstone in a letter in
February, 1870, that "on all these points they are very decided and unanimous," and that they had "openly staked their influence over the people
in the confidence of a satisfactory Land Bill."[65] Once the priests had
engendered such confidence in the peasants, it was not difficult to get
their cooperation in the fight for a denominational university. To this
end, Michael J. McCarthy wrote:

> One of my earliest recollections is the
> sight of a crowd of men--chiefly farmers--
> and many widows waiting round a table outside
> the chapel door to sign a petition for a
> Catholic University (in 1873); the priest
> himself commanding the people to sign.[66]

To the priests, the establishment of a Catholic university was of
first importance. For instance, McCarthy further tells that "when any
other petition was placed for signature outside the chapel, it was not
with the approval of the parish priest."[67] The university question seemed
to be at the center of the priests' activities, as they pressed their
demands for equality. One avenue through which the priests sought the
achievement of religious equality was through the promotion of a chartered
and endowed Catholic university in addition to Maynooth College. Another
means was by way of a solution to the land problem whereby Protestant
ascendancy in higher education could be curtailed. The effect of the
Land Bills since 1870 on Trinity College was to bring about a gradual
fulfillment of these ends.

---

[65]Gladstone Papers, B.M. Add. MS. 44249, f. 135, Manning to
Gladstone, February 5, 1870, as quoted by E. R. Norman, op.cit., p. 396.

[66]M. J. McCarthy, op,cit., p. 33.

[67]Ibid.

The Tenants Purchase Act (Ireland), 1873, was instrumental in speeding up land purchase.[68] As a result of this and subsequent land purchase acts, Trinity College experienced a heavy loss of income on the sale of her agrarian rights. So severe was this loss, that by 1903, an annual sum of £5,000 out of the Irish Development Grant had to be given to Trinity College as compensation. The University Commission of 1904 was appointed to look into this matter, and Mr. Jellett, in giving evidence, pointed out that the loss "could not be compensated by the £5,000 a year."[69]

If the assumption holds that the loss of income from Trinity College was naturally followed by a corresponding loss of power, prestige, and indulgence, then the land question seemed as important as the Church question to the Catholics in their struggle for equality in higher education. No wonder, then, that Dr. C. W. Russell, President of Maynooth College, writing to Gladstone in February, 1870, stated that he regarded the Land Bill of 1870 "as a greater success even than the Church Bill."[70] No wonder, also, that the Irish Catholic hierarchy had been devoting so much energy to the land question; for the significance of that question to the university education question can hardly be over-emphasized.

Very often the size of endowments for higher or intermediate education was determined by the amount and value of land. This fact was emphasized by the Commissioners of Education in Ireland in their 1854-55 report. The Commissioners admitted that the management of the estates forming the endowments of certain of the schools necessarily occupied much of their time; they further complained that the necessary outlay for the upkeep of the schools was conditioned by the small endowments which consisted "of rents derived from their respective estates."[71] Much of the success of education, therefore, was directly related to the fortunes of the land.

---

[68] Great Britain, <u>Parliamentary Papers</u>, 1873, II, 285, "A Bill to provide facilities for the purchase of Lands by Tenants in Ireland and amend and alter Part II and Part III of the Landlord and Tenant (Ireland) act of 1870," pp. 1-9.

[69] Great Britain, <u>Parliamentary Papers</u>, 1905, XXVII, 81, Trinity College, Dublin, Estates Commission, 1904," Minutes of Evidence, p. 9.

[70] Gladstone Papers, B.M. Add. MS. 44425, Russell to Gladstone, February 18, 1870, as quoted by E. R. Norman, <u>op.cit.</u>, p. 397.

[71] Great Britain, <u>Parliamentary Papers</u>, 1854-55, XVI, 23, "Annual Report of the Commissioners of Education in Ireland to his Excellency the Lord Lieutenant for the year 1854-55," p. 1.

After 1879, the trend was in the direction of procuring more land for educational purposes. Catholic agitation for land purchase in the preceding decade and after was not to be in vain. Not only had the Government stepped up its efforts in passing general land purchase acts, but it also tried to improve the opportunities for land purchase for educational purpose by non-Protestant groups. The bill of 1883 recognized the failure of the 1855 land-lease act in this respect, and sought to correct it:

> Whereas difficulties have been experienced in obtaining leases under such an Act,... it is desirable to enable all recognized religious congregations to purchase lands for the purposes aforesaid (i.e., erect suitable buildings for religious worship and for the residence of their clergymen, ministers, and pastors, and school houses for the education of their children), and for the obtaining of residences for schoolmasters for all schools in Ireland.[72]

How heartened the Irish Catholics must have been by this Act!

---

[72] Ibid., 1883, IX, 259, "A Bill to afford Increased Facilities for obtaining Sites for Places of Worship, Schools and Residences for Teachers and Clergymen in Ireland," p. 1.

CHAPTER IV

THE UNIVERSITY EDUCATION PROBLEM

For many years the Irish Catholics saw themselves at a great disadvantage in the existing system of higher education. While many of them genuinely recognized and appreciated the work of the University of Dublin or Trinity College in the education of eminent Irishmen, they were never satisfied with its exclusive control by members of the Irish Anglican Church. Some leading Protestants, however, praised Trinity College for its work in the education of Catholics. William Plunkett, who became Anglican Archbishop of Dublin in 1884, asserted in the House of Commons in 1870 that "many of the Roman Catholic gentlemen who now filled the highest official and judicial positions in Ireland, obtained their education and their degrees in Trinity College, Dublin."[1] But the Catholics themselves felt differently.

Intense Catholic agitation for an improved system of higher education in Ireland dates from 1865. The drastic change in Irish opinion was created by the coming of Cardinal Cullen as Archbishop of Dublin in 1862. Cullen soon pronounced as not worthy to receive the sacraments of the Catholic Church those parents and guardians who allowed their children to attend the Queen's Colleges at Belfast, Cork, and Galway. These three colleges comprising the Queen's University, founded in 1845, were non-sectarian. Opposition, from time to time, came from both Anglican Protestants and Roman Catholics. Under the influence of Cardinal Cullen, many Catholic bishops throughout the 1860's denounced the Queen's Colleges as godless and graceless institutions, which in their view represented the indifferentism and infidelity of modern society. Henceforth, Catholic dissatisfaction grew apace.

On June 20, 1865, The O'Donoghue, Member of Parliament for Tipperary, moved in the Commons that her Majesty be presented with an address, bringing to her notice the conscientious objections of Roman Catholics to the system of University Education in Ireland. O'Donoghue said that the position of Catholics was "one of grievous

---

[1] Great Britain, 3 Hansard's Parliamentary Debates, CC 1870, p. 1099.

inferiority."[2] He went on to show that while 600,000 Anglican Protestants had adequate arrangements for university training, over four-and-a-half million Catholics did not enjoy such privileges. In Belfast, the total number of students was 405, of whom there were only 22 Catholics, in Cork there were 123 Catholics out of a total of 263, in Galway there were in all 169 students, the Catholics numbering 78, and at Trinity College there were only 45 Catholic students among the one-thousand enrolled. Of an aggregate of 1,837 students registered in the legally recognized colleges, 268 were Catholics.[3] O'Donoghue, voicing the opinion of many Catholic leaders, suggested that the remedy for this ill-balanced situation would be the granting of a Charter to the Catholic University in Dublin, thereby giving it the power to confer degrees.

So finally, the Catholic University was founded in 1854 in an attempt to fill the void in the higher educational system. John Henry Newman was appointed its first head. Four archbishops and two other prelates from each province comprised the Board of the new university which consisted of the faculties of theology, law, medicine, belles-lettres, and science. The government of the university was conducted by a committee of archbishops and bishops who met once a year. No financial or other support from the State was received, its maintenance being exclusively by voluntary offerings. The complete academic course was to extend over seven years and was designed to meet the needs of all its students. During the first two years, the students would concentrate on classics, ancient history, mathematics and logic. The next two years were devoted to courses in modern history, political economy, law, and metaphysics, leading to the Bachelor's Degree. Superior students were to remain for three more years aimed at the Master's Degree in Letters or Science, or the Doctorate in the three higher faculties of Theology, Law, and Medicine. The unity of the Catholic dogma and spirit was the permeating force in the life and teaching of the university.

By having their own institution, the Catholics felt that they had the best chance of preserving the faith and morals of their youth. They had complained bitterly of the evils of mixed education,

---

[2] Great Britain, 3 Hansard's Parliamentary Debates, CLXXX (1865), p. 542.

[3] Ibid., p. 543.

and held that secular instruction in metaphysics, moral philosophy, and kindred subjects could not by any conceivable method of interpretation be given to united classes of Protestants and Catholics without wounding the religious susceptibilities of one or the other. The Irish Catholic bishops made it clear in 1869 that they considered that the Catholic people of Ireland had a right to a university of their own, although they did not insist that recognition of this right was indispensable to the settlement of the university question. They would accept a National University, on the London University model, with the power to examine and confer degrees.[4] They demanded that a distinct Catholic College be affiliated to it, that both Catholics and Protestants alike share in university honors and emoluments, and that there be proper representation of Catholics in the Senate. The bishops' demands were important in the long struggle to resolve the university education question in Ireland.

The higher education problem in Ireland was characterized by religious as well as educational inequality. Matters became even more complicated as the Catholics pressed for a consideration of the whole system of education in Ireland rather than the university education question alone. They complained that conditions in their schools at both primary and secondary level were also quite unsatisfactory. Public funds were used only very sparingly for the maintenance of these schools. Consequently, the school buildings were old and dilapidated, school supplies inadequate for the most part, and their teachers were poorly qualified and badly paid. Above all, the Catholics resented having their children taught by Anglican teachers whom they feared might convert them to Protestantism. For this reason the Irish Catholics treasured highly the education work carried on by the Christian Brothers, a lay order of Catholic teachers, established by Edmund Rice in 1804. The Irish Catholic bishops were satisfied that the Brothers were conscientiously trying to impart to youthful Catholic minds the correct impressions resulting from both secular and religious knowledge. There was always great concern for preparatory education, at both primary and secondary level.

The lack of proper secondary education was viewed by Catholics as unfair, in light of the advantages enjoyed by the Protestant endowed schools. A Royal Commission appointed to examine the Irish endowed schools in 1858 concluded that Catholic conditions could

---

[4] The Nation IX September, 1869, p. 242.

not be met by simply rearranging the existing endowments for Irish intermediate education. But the bishops were not all pleased to read in the Commissioners' Report that "the provision for local management would enable the trustees to make suitable regulations for religious instruction, provided that the school as a condition of its partaking of the grant of public money admit of the united education of all religious persuasions, and provided, also, that the local managers be subject to the direct control of the proposed Board of Commissioners of Endowed Schools."[5] The bishops desired separate Catholic schools, and in cases where their schools received some form of grant-in-aid, such as the 112 conventual and monastic schools connected to the National Board in 1859, they wished for little or no State interference. They often complained that the State had done very little to promote Irish Catholic secondary education.

Charges against the State for neglect of Catholic secondary education were by no means unfounded. The early Stuarts made efforts to establish secondary education in Ireland on a large scale. They founded the "Free Royal Schools," as they have been called, at Armagh, Cavan, Dungannon, Portora, and Raphoe, and endowed them with lands worth about £6,000 per year. For a time these schools seemed even to rival Eton, Winchester, and the other great public schools in England. But although these schools were nominally open to different creeds, they became, nevertheless, under Protestant ascendancy in the eighteenth century, restricted to the youth of that faith. It was not until after the relaxation of the penal code in 1829 that the Irish Catholics began to found secondary schools; and although these schools received no State aid for a long time, some of them did excellent work. The efforts of Catholic leaders in this regard must be considered praiseworthy. In Ulster, the Presbyterians established a number of secondary schools, some of which received state aid.

On the whole, however, the progress made by secondary schools in Ireland had been slow. This has mainly been due to three reasons: the Irish aristocrats usually sent their sons to be educated in the great public schools in England; Irish secondary schools have seldom been well endowed; the middle class in Ireland has always been very small and could exert only a little influence. Indeed, Irish secondary schools had been decidedly inferior to what they ought to have been. The

---

[5] Great Britain, <u>Parliamentary Papers</u>, Vol. XXII, Part I (Reports from Commissioners, Vol. V 2886-I), February, 1858, "Endowed Schools, Ireland Commission," p. 278.

Commission of 1878 appointed to examine secondary education in Ireland, reported, like the Commission of 1854, a far from favorable account of the system. In 1871, out of a total population of 5,500,000 only 10,814 boys in Ireland were receiving instruction in Latin, Greek or modern languages. In England about ten or fifteen out of every 1,000 boys were instructed in these languages, while in Ireland only two in every 1,000 enjoyed similar privileges. Moreover, in such poor situations the Catholics were always at a greater disadvantage. In 1878 there were 199 in every 100,000 Protestants in Ireland obtaining secondary training, but of every 100,000 Catholics only two were being educated in the endowed secondary schools.[6]

Such inadequate secondary preparation for Catholic youth was of grave concern to the Irish Catholics, for it meant a further undermining of their university education. In 1873, as in 1859, one of the main episocpal educational grievances was that the lack of proper secondary schools for Catholics was giving an unfair advantage to Protestant students who were provided with well endowed schools. The Catholic leaders had pleaded with Gladstone not to restrict his attention to universities alone, but also to include intermediate education. For that matter, Gladstone himself was fully conscious of the needs in this area. In fact he spoke first of intermediate education as the House met in committee in February, 1873, to consider Irish University education. Gladstone referred to intermediate education as "a subject of great importance," but insisted that it must arise "as a necessary consequence of the legislation which Parliament may think fit to adopt with respect to the question of University education."[7]

The need for higher education reform was highlighted by scholars in the early twentieth century. William O'Connor Morris voiced the sentiments of the scholars when he made the following observation:

> The extreme unfairness of this University system, the ascendancy secured by Trinity College, which, admirable institution as it was, was practically nearly confined to Protestants of the upper class; the failure, with respect to Catholic Ireland, of the Queen's Colleges and Queen's University,

---

[6] Great Britain, 3 Hansard's Parliamentary Debates, CCXLI, p. 436.

[7] Great Britain, Parliamentary Papers, 1873, CCXIV, p. 379.

> and...above all the denial to the Catholic
> University of any share in the bounty of
> the State..., attracted the attention of
> several statesmen between 1850 and 1870
> but nothing was done or even attempted.[8]

Gladstone decided to attempt a solution of the university education problem during his first ministry, 1868-1874, but that was not going to be an easy task. The seeming little ripples on the surface associated with Maynooth College at the time of the Irish Church Act would develop into whirlpools when the Ministry came to the very difficult problem of university education. Indeed, the experiences of the past must have taught him that this third branch of the Upas Tree was, as Justin McCarthy correctly observed, "a branch of tougher fibre, well calculated to turn the edge of even the best weapon, and to jar the strongest arm that wielded it."[9]

McCarthy had correctly perceived that the whole university question was to become increasingly difficult throughout the period 1869-1879. The Irish Catholic hierarchy somewhat disillusioned with disestablishment as a solution to the education question, took the matter into their hands vigorously during this time. The Catholics soon realized that Protestant ascendancy had only been minimized with the passing of the Irish Church Act. The thrust of this ascendancy had been too great for too long for any drastic change to be effected in a short time. Many supporters of the Establishment in 1869 went as far as to imply that there could be no real disestablishment of the Irish Anglican Church. The view of many critics was strongly expressed in the Blackwood's Magazine:

> So long as the Church of England subsists
> in England its real disestablishment in Ireland
> is simply impossible. It may lose the parish
> Church, the glebe, and the tithes; but it will
> continue as a congregation, as a body of Church
> of England men living together in Church association, and it will bring in the State into every
> town or village in which they dwell.[10]

---

[8] W. Morris, <u>Present Irish Questions</u> (London: Grant Richards, 1901), p. 343.

[9] Justin McCarthy, <u>A History of Our Own Times</u> (New York: United States Book Company, 1895), IV, p. 556.

[10] "Mr. Gladstone and Disestablishment," <u>Blackwood's Magazine</u>, CV (February, 1869), p. 243.

If the strength and influence of the Establishment was going to be continued to be felt in Church affairs, it was not going to be less felt in educational matters. For instance, William Morris pointed to a few secondary schools--St. Columba was much the best--which had been founded "usually for the benefit of the late Established Church."[11] Moreover, in their declearation of March, 1870, relating to academical education, the Heads of the Roman Catholic church expressed consciousness of a lingering Protestant ascendancy in the educational system:

> We believe that the sectarian virulence, which unhappily prevails in Ireland is in a great measure due to the maintenance for so long a time of ecclesiastical ascendancy, which the legislature has wisely abolished, and to the fact that educational equality has not yet been granted to the Roman Catholics of Ireland.[12]

The Catholics, therefore, properly recognized the fact that Protestant ascendancy had not been sufficiently affected by legislation designed to bring about educational equality, and this was of paramount concern to them.

Catholic concern for educational equality was paralleled by their concern for the type of secular education then prevalent; and here, again, disestablishment had disappointed their hopes. The report of the Intermediate Education Board for the year 1879 referred to the role of the Irish Church Act in the promotion of secular education:

> It was provided by the Act (Intermediate Education (Ireland) Act, 1878) that the Commissioners of Church Temporalities in Ireland, should, out of the property accruing to the Commissioners under the Irish Church Act, 1869,... provide for the use of the Board either in cash or in securities or rent charges of an equivalent value,

---

[11] W. Morris, op.cit., p. 337.

[12] Great Britain, Parliamentary Papers, 1870, LIV, 601, "Copy of Declaration of Heads of Roman Catholic Colleges and Schools and Other Persons lately laid before the Prime Minister," p. 1.

> such amount not exceeding in the whole one
> million of pounds sterling...to be applied
> in the promotion of secular education...[13]

The conflict surrounding secular education was a never-ending one. It was very closely identified with united or mixed education, which the Anglicans staunchly supported, and the Catholics strongly opposed. Although the Government was reluctant to admit it, the hostility of the Catholic community was a factor which influenced the decision not to extend the system of Model Schools. These were a type of secondary schools to which Catholics vehemently objected as endangering the faith and morals of their youth. On June 19, 1866, the Chief Secretary for Ireland, Chichester Fortescue, wrote to the Commissioners on National Education outlining certain changes which embodied the establishment of Model Schools under local control.[14] The new provisions for the model schools included residences for Chaplins of different denominations, and denominational boarding houses for students.

The Model School Board accepted the new provisions relating to denominational aspects. Nevertheless, in their letter of approval to Fortescue, the board members refused to commit themselves to adopting any particular details, making it clear that while they were ready to cooperate with the Government in carrying out the proposals, they had also decided to keep "always in view the principles of united secular education."[15] Their action was characteristic of Protestant determination to uphold the mixed system of education.

However, the Catholics were not going to relinquish their struggle against the mixed system, since it would become even more intensified in the sphere of higher education. The Catholics regarded the combination of secular and sectarian education at Trinity College as a great evil. To them, as Maguire expressed in the debate on the condition of Ireland in 1868,

---

[13] Great Britain, Parliamentary Papers, 1880, XXIII, 31, "Report of the Intermediate Education Board for the year 1879," p. 3.

[14] Ibid., 1866, 213, "Correspondence between Her Majesty's Government and the Commissioners of National Education (Ireland) on the Subject of the Organization and Government of Training and Model Schools," pp. 1-3.

[15] Ibid., p. 3.

Trinity College seemed "a monstrous anomaly."[16] Maguire laid the blame for this anomaly at Trinity College to the roots of the Establishment. Moreover, he declared that there was "no justification for the existence of this anomaly-- the Church Establishment in Ireland."[17]

In March, 1870, the Irish Ecclesiastical Record, which was established in 1864 by Cardinal Cullen to propagate Roman influence and practice, commented on the mixed system:

> A system in which Catholicity with its strict morality, its numerous religious observances and its clearly defined dogmas, has everything to lose, while Protestantism with its freedom from religious restraints and its lattitude in tolerating doctrinal errors finds the very atmosphere filled with the ideas, the principles and the sentiments it loves.[18]

Such pronouncements were designed to keep Catholics from the Queen's Colleges as well as from Trinity College, although some Catholics held the latter as the lesser of the two evils.

Trinity College continued to be a Protestant stronghold even after disestablishment. T. W. Moody, in a brilliant article on the Irish university question in the nineteenth century, pointed to the continued influence of the Irish Anglican Church at Trinity College, despite disestablishment:

> Though disestablishment, in 1869, put it on a footing of legal equality with all other churches in Ireland, it continued to be identified with the landed aristocracy and the professions and to occupy throughout the nineteenth century a dominant position in society and the state. Irish Churchmen

---

[16] Great Britain, 3 Hansard's Parliamentary Debates, 1868, CXC, p. 1308.

[17] Ibid., p. 1307.

[18] Irish Ecclesiastical Record, new series, VI, 1869-70, p. 256.

> regarded Trinity College as their peculiar
> sphere;...they were in general determined to
> maintain its traditional Anglican character.[19]

Protestant determination to maintain the traditional Anglican character of Trinity College, was facilitated not only by the continuation of religious tests, but also by united secular education which provided loopholes for proselytism. It is not surprising, therefore, that the petition of certain graduates of Trinity College in 1870 bore a strong conservative note, that "in any legislation affecting University Education in Ireland, the Protestant Constitution of the University of Dublin may be preserved unimpaired; and that the Protestant People of Ireland may not be deprived of privileges which they have enjoyed, without interruption, for 300 years."[20]

Nor were the Provost and Fellows of Trinity College less vociferous in their defence of mixed education. Their attitutde toward the increased demands of the Catholic hierarchy for a system of denominational colleges is revealed in the following statement:

> Concurring as under the altered circumstances
> of the country we feel bound to do, in the
> expediency of this measure, we believe that
> the overthrow of the system of united education
> and the establishment as has been proposed, of
> denominational colleges in its place, would be
> a retrograde step in national policy, injurious
> to sound learning in Ireland, subversive to true
> freedom.[21]

While to the Protestants true freedom was assoicated with united secular education, to the Catholics true freedom meant unrestricted control of their own religious education. In the 1870's, Catholic desire for such control was no less strong than it was in the 1860's.

---

[19] *History*, Vol. XLIII, No. 148, June, 1958, p. 91.

[20] Great Britain, *Parliamentary Papers*, 1870, LIV, 637, "Petition of Certain Graduates of the University of Trinity College, Dublin, to the Honourable, the Commons of the United Kingdom of Great Britain and Ireland in Parliament assembled," p. 3.

[21] *Ibid*.

The Catholic bishops never ceased to press their demands for their own schools, at all levels, free from State control or intervention. Disestablishment, with its emphasis on religious freedom, had strengthened their position. Educational freedom was the burden of the pastoral letter of the Irish bishops on mixed education on October 20, 1871:

> As religious equality which according to the constitution of this country is our inalienable right, is incomplete without educational freedom and equality, we demand as a right that, in all the approaching legislation on the subject of education, the principle of educational equality shall be acted upon.[22]

It was clear from their pastoral letter of 1871 on mixed education, that the Irish bishops had not retreated from their demands for the abolition of the system of mixed education. Then, according to the Edinburgh Review in January, 1872, the bishops would never cease to oppose to the outmost of their power, the Model Schools, Queen's Colleges, Trinity College, and all similar institutions dangerous to the faith and morals of Catholics."[23] In the sphere of primary education the bishops demanded that in all exclusive Catholic schools "there shall be the removal of all restrictions upon religious instruction, so that the fullness of religious teaching may enter into the course of daily secular education with full liberty for the use of Catholic books and religious emblems, and for the performance of religious exercises."[24] With regard to intermediate education, the hierarchy wished to see all existing endowments whether derived from Protestant or Catholic bounty, put into a common fund, and applied to open scholarships or grants on the principle of payments by results. On the subject of university education, their language appeared quite guarded,

---

[22] Patrick Moran (ed.), The Pastoral Letters and Other Writings of Cardinal Cullen (Dublin: Browne and Nolan, 1882), III, p. 407.

[23] "Irish University Education," Edinburgh Review, Vol. 135, Jan., 1872, p. 167.

[24] Ibid.

however. The Saturday Review observed that "the resolutions which related to higher education were unexpectedly moderate in their wording."[25]

But while it must be admitted that the bishops were very cautious in wording their higher education demands at that time, it must not be forgotten that the principle had not been changed. So far, the bishops had been least successful with the university education question which, as Morley stated, "stood in the front rank of unsettled questions."[26] The bishops had seen the collapse of the Mayo plan in 1868, and they had become aware of Gladstone's lack of interest in endowing a Catholic university. Their new demands indicated only that they decided on a milder approach to achieve their goal.

Consequently, the Bishops' Resolutions of 1871 contained no specific demand for the establishment of a separate Roman Catholic College or University. It is true that they still asserted their right to have a Catholic University endowed by the State. But they expressed willingness to agree to the alternative of having one National University, with one or more colleges, conducted upon purely Catholic principles, and at the same time, with provisions for full Catholic participation in the privileges enjoyed by other colleges, of whatever denomination and character. For the security of Catholic principles, the bishops insisted on having "full control in all things regarding faith and morals."[27] Furthermore, the bishops demanded that the Catholic interests be "adequately represented upon the Senate, or other supreme University Body, by persons enjoying the confidence of the Catholic bishops, priests, and people of Ireland."[28]

The Edinburgh Review did not hesitate to seek to link the bishops' claims with the after-effects of disestablishment in a critical comment in 1872:

---

[25] "Irish Education," Saturday Review, Vol. XXXIII, 1872, p. 72.

[26] John Morley, The Life of William Ewart Gladstone (New York: The MacMillan Company, 1911), II, 434.

[27] "Irish University Education," Edinburgh Review, 1872, Vol. CXXXV, p. 168.

[28] Ibid.

> The bishops seem to think, however, that
> religious equality justifies the demand that
> Roman Catholics shall enjoy large educational
> endowments now, on the ground that the members
> of the Irish Church had already enjoyed them
> for centuries...But..., if the State has thought
> fit to take away the privilege of exclusive
> Universities from the religion of the majority
> in England, it can hardly be expected to found
> an exclusive University for the religion of the
> majority in Ireland.[29]

In England, where the Establishment still existed, the trend was away from denominational education. The Cowper Temple Clause of the Education Act of 1870 stipulated that in the public elementary schools neither religious catechism nor religious formulary distinctive of any particular denomination was to be taught.[30] After 1870, no cognizance of religious instruction was taken by the State. During this time, too, certain statutes were passed to effect changes in higher education.

Statutes passed at both Oxford and Cambridge in 1869 allowed persons to become members of the universities without joining any College, provided that they lived in licensed buildings, and were subject to a special board. In 1871, the Universities Test Act was passed abolishing all oaths and affirmations at Oxford, Cambridge, and Durham. The principles of that act were applied to all areas of study except Divinity, and included professorships, fellowships, scholarships, and emoluments of all kinds, as well as matriculation and degrees.[31] Meanwhile, Protestant critics of Catholic demands for denominational education were quick to note the inconsistency of opening up Oxford and Cambridge in England, and then to endow new colleges with even more stringent tests in Ireland. A few Roman

---

[29] Ibid., p. 180.

[30] Great Britain, Parliamentary Papers, 1870, I, 583, "A Bill to Provide for Public Elementary Education in England and Wales," p. 6.

[31] Great Britain, Parliamentary Papers, 1871, VI, 535, "University Test Act, 1871," p. 2.

Catholics also seemed to have shared this view. Prominent among these was one Mr. Quill, a Roman Catholic graduate of Trinity College, Dublin. Late in 1871 he delivered an address before the Historical Society of that College, in which he stated among other things that the religion of the majority in England can no longer claim a university for itself, but majority and minority alike must seek the same knowledge from the same fountains. Quill then posed a very significant question: "On what principles, then, can the religion of the majority in Ireland claim that which the Imperial Parliament has thought fit to take away from the religion of the majority in England?"[32]

Such sentiments as Mr. Quill's reveal the parallel situation which existed between the educational problems in England and in Ireland. The view has often been expressed that the statutory changes affecting university reform in England had their roots in the Irish situation. This idea has been upheld by W. O. Chadwick in his book Westcott and the University in which he mentions Dr. Pusey's proposal to the Wesleyan Conference of 1868 for concurrent endowment of denominational colleges at English universities.[33] The movement for concurrent endowment was arrested by Gladstone's resolutions on the Irish Church in May, 1868, which were intended to put a stop to all chances of concurrent endowment in universities as well as churches in Ireland. Further, suggestions to open Trinity College fellowships to all religious denominations constituted Irish precedents for England. These precedents had been very largely affected by the sequence of events, the most important of which was the disestablishment of the Irish Church. The position of Trinity College was to be greatly affected thereby.

Some scholars even predicted that the events following disestablishment would, within four decades, see a gradual unfolding of the non-sectarian principle at Trinity College. This view was expressed in 1869 by Professor J. B. Quinlan, Dean of the Faculty of Medicine of the Catholic University and formerly Sizar of Trinity College, Dublin:

---

[32] "The Irish University Question," Edinburgh Review, Vol. 135, Jan., 1872, p. 181.

[33] W. O. Chadwick, Westcott and the University, Cambridge, 1963, pp. 11-12.

> Should the Legislature convert into law
> the motion of Professor Fawcett, the condition
> of Trinity College will gradually change by a
> movement of almost geological imperceptibility.
> Taking into consideration the comparative slow-
> ness of promotion consequent upon the disestab-
> lishment of the Church...I have calculated that...
> the next generation will see a pretty equal
> mixture of Junior Fellows of all or no religion.[34]

But the Catholic hierarchy held another view. Cardinal Cullen's pastoral of September, 1869, proposed the splitting up of Trinity College as well as the Queen's Colleges into denominational institutions, and the appropriation of some of the funds of Trinity College to the Catholic University.[35] In addition, the bishops' demands at the time likewise called for an end to Trinity College as a place of mixed education.[36]

The difference in viewpoint over what was to be the outcome of Trinity College, was symbolic of the conflicting interpretations of the principles of disestablishment. In essence disestablishment signified religious liberty and religious equality. When these principles touched upon education, then it was expected that there would be religious equality in educational opportunity. To the Protestants, this would come to mean equal chances in a mixed educational system regardless of religion. The authorities at Trinity College quickly realized that the College could no longer maintain its former position when disestablishment became effective, and consented, despite some underlying currents of conservatism, to relinquish the denominational character of the College. For while Trinity College was not directly referred to in the resolutions on the Irish Church, Gladstone did not fail to intimate that insofar as it was an appendage of the Church, it would in the end receive consideration similar to that of Maynooth. During the debate on March 30, 1868, he emphatically stated, "I feel almost an equal confidence that the

---

[34] The Times, September 8, 1869, p. 4.

[35] Ibid., September 4, 1869, p. 7.

[6] Ibid., September 4, 1869, p. 6.

very same...judgment which goes to the Church would go likewise to that which is inseparably connected with the Church."[37] It was over this principle that Gladstone and C. W. Russell, the President of Maynooth College, had disagreements.

When Dr. Russell disagreed with Mr. Gladstone, holding that Maynooth should be treated as an educational rather than an ecclesiastical establishment, he was reflecting the trend of Catholic thinking on the meaning and implication of disestablishment. Such thought was to guide their actions as they sought for a solution to the university question, in the decade after 1869. It would seem that the Catholics had seriously hoped that an acceptable answer to the education difficulty would accompany the settlement of the Church question; to them; as to the Protestants, disestablishment connoted religious liberty and religious equality. But unlike the Protestants, the Catholics construed disestablishment to mean freedom to pursue their own system of education under conditions equal to that of Protestants. Educational as well as religious equality for Catholics was the keynote of a letter addressed to the National Association by the Bishop of Ross in 1868:

> Justice will compel any Government selected by Her Majesty to grant a charter to our Catholic University of Ireland and to place it on a footing similar to...other educational establishments... these are measures which once that we become freed from the isolated and disadvantageous position into which we have been thrown as Catholics must be conceded to us for the sake of religious liberty and religious equality.[38]

In their struggle for religious liberty and equality, the Irish Catholics found strong support in the English Dissenters. Both had suffered common disabilities resulting from the Establishment and thus had united for disestablishment. Both groups were in accord on disestablishment and disendowment of the Irish Anglican Church; the Dissenters hoped that this would set a precedent for similar action in England, and for Irish Catholic support in such an event. Both groups had promoted the voluntary principle. Peculiar

---

[37] Great Britain, 3 Hansard's Parliamentary Debates, CXCI, 1868, p. 475.

[38] The Times, April 10, 1868, p. 8.

circumstances soon strained relationship, however, and this augured badly for the Irish university education question. The close association was bound to be temporary because of strong anti-Catholic feelings among English Dissenters, and soon after disestablishment, a great gulf was apparent. Like the Anglican Protestants, the Dissenters became exasperated by Vatican Decrees, Papal Infallibility, and the Ultramontane claims of the Irish Catholic bishops.

The education question in general and the university problem in particular became the focal point of disagreement between the Irish Catholics and English Dissenters. The two issues with which Dissenters as well as Catholics were mainly concerned were disestablishment and education, and indeed neither of these was considered in isolation. Hence, the Nonconformists took careful note of the developing trend of Catholic educational demands following disestablishment. Although the Nonconformists had supported the Catholics over religious equality, they warned that they would strongly oppose the implementation of the bishops' resolutions of September, 1869, dealing with education.

Even before disestablishment, the uneasy cooperation between the English Dissenters and Irish Catholics was threatened by educational matters. The Dissenters were members of the English Liberation Society. Since 1862 the Liberationists had become seriously concerned with the position of Maynooth. In 1859, they held it to be indissolubly connected with the Church question, a stand which some leading Catholics were to oppose later. The Dissenters had even hinted that until Irish Catholics could be induced to give up the Maynooth endowment, the Establishment question would be in jeopardy. But they showed themselves quite flexible when they refrained from agitating against Maynooth in an attempt to cement the alliance with the Irish Catholics, an which did not last very long. One reason for this short lived alliance was that the Dissenters were disappointed that, after the Irish Church disestablishment, the Irish Catholics showed no interest in overthrowing the Established Church in England.

With regard to disestablishment in England, William Monsell, Member of Parliament for Limerick, declared in the Commons in 1869 that the Irish considered it unworthy of them to attempt, "upon any religious ground, to overthrow that which the (English) nation had established."[39] When in 1871 Edward

---

[39] Great Britain, 3 <u>Hansard's Parliamentary Debates</u>, 1869, CXCVI, p. 1024.

Miall, Member of Parliament for Bradford, introduced a bill for English Disestablishment into the Commons, based on Irish precedent,[40] it was in vain that the Dissenters appealed for help from the Irish. The working agreement of the 1860's was unfulfilled by the Irish Catholics, thus bringing to a rupture the union between them and the Dissenters. The situation then deteriorated as the underlying division over the university question found expression in the 1870's.

Like the Irish Catholics, the English Dissenters considered that they were not given equal educational opportunity. In 1873, the Blackwood's Magazine observed that "there is not a chance of Dissenting schools obtaining, by fair competition, anything like an equal influence with the schools of the Establishment," and therefore they wished to "pull down the Church."[41] But the Dissenters also saw another kind of inequality in the Catholic demands for an education based on Catholic wishes and desires. The Dissenters considered the Catholic demands in Ireland just as peremptory as the actions of the Established Church in England. According to the Blackwood's Magazine, the Dissenters had "objected to the Lion's share, and (were) not going to tolerate that of the wolf."[42]

Nonconformity, by its very nature, was firmly set against Romanism, and for many years the Dissenters or Nonconformists proclaimed their anti-Romanism in many different ways. The education question provided the Dissenters with an avenue for opposing Catholicism, for the Nonconformist views on education were quite unlike those of the Catholics. The Nonconformists declared against concurrent endowment and denominationalism in education which the Catholics wanted. They also favored secularization and united education which the Catholics frowned upon.

The Catholics had thus learnt from experience that support from the Dissenters or Nonconformists, so freely given at the time of the disestablishment of the Irish Church would not be carried over into the university question. In 1868, the Dublin Review expressed caution over the uneasy alliance between Catholics and Dissenters when it warned that the unfortunate aspect of the Church question was the

---

[40]Annual Register, 1871 (History), p. 92.

[41]"Our State and Prospects," Blackwood's Magazine, 1973, CXIII, p. 252.

[42]Ibid.

close connection that had developed between Irish Catholics and English Liberals.[43] This fact raises questions concerning the nature of the relationship between the Church question and the problem of university education. In 1874, Jonathan Pim addressed the equality issue in the context of the relationship between the Church question and the university question:

> If equality is to be produced by levelling down, after the precedent set by the Church Act, it must be complete, the revenues of Trinity College must be confiscated, and applied to other purposes. If equality is to be produced by levelling up, the maintenance of education, like that of religious worship, must be voluntary, without any endowment on the part of the State.[44]

The role of the State after disestablishment was indeed one of the difficult aspects of the university education question. Pim's remarks on this debatable issue reveal the magnitude of the difficulty:

> In the disestablishment of the Church, the State has declared that it will not, for the future, make itself (responsible) in any way for the celebration of religious worship in Ireland. But its policy as respects education has been directly the reverse. Both in England and Ireland, it has, year after year, taken increased interest in educational matters.[45]

This anomalous position of the State was a major problem for the Catholics who had hoped that disestablishment would solve the university question. After disestablishment, the State fully adopted the principle that it was

---

[43]"The Irish Establishment," Dublin Review, New Series, Vol. XI, July, 1868, p. 252.

[44]Jonathan Pim, The Irish University Question (Dublin: Hodges, Foster and Co., 1874), p. 12.

[45]Ibid.

its duty to provide the means of education for every individual. However, the philosophy of the State in education, largely imbued with secular impulses and indifferentism, was to be in conflict with that of the Catholic hierarchy which embraced education as a work of religion.

The question of equality of educational opportunity, therefore, seemed as equally remote after disestablishment as before. For if the colleges were to be secularized, according to Acts of Parliament and College Statutes, then a decided advantage was given to those whose interest was in secular learning over those who believed that all education ought to be associated with and influenced by religion. Further, it was going to be difficult to effect educational equality through religious equality. The Church Act of 1869 had disestablished and disendowed the Irish Church, placing all the religious bodies in Ireland on the same level. But the University of Dublin had neither been disestablished nor disendowed, and the course that was contemplated would hardly result in putting all sects or persons on the same level. Needless to say, the principles of disestablishment and disendowment applied to the university would not have solved the problem, so that, if privileges and endowments were taken away from all institutions established for imparting higher education, none could complain of inequality. In addition, since universal disendowment was not in keeping with the spirit of the age, the greatest danger then lay in partiality of treatment of the problem of university education by the Protestants.

Many Protestant leaders were in deep conflict over the university problem in Ireland. The disestablishment of the Irish Church had opened their eyes to the danger in which their exclusive privileges in regard to university education were placed. The Protestants were convinced that those privileges could no longer be openly retained. Consequently they sought practical ways of privately perpetuating them while theoretically abandoning them. The misfortunes which the Church had suffered provided enough reasons for resisting further aggression from the Catholics. It was a serious state of affairs. When, therefore, Gladstone wrote to the President of Maynooth in January, 1873, concerning the university education problem it was in an atmosphere of uncertainty:

> We are approaching a great and critical question, and the redemption of our last pledge, though not the fulfillment of our last duty, for duty can never cease. If we fail, I think it will not be from an inadequate sense of the character of our engagement, nor from want of pains, nor

from what is called the fear of man. From the nature of the case in part, but more from the temper of men's minds on this particular question, no plan can be proposed which will not attract much criticism.[46]

Gladstone and his Ministry had become more and more conscious of the increasing difficulty and complexities of the university education problem. They were so wary in their approach to it, that according to John Morley, "no communications were opened with the bishops beforehand, probably from a surmise that they were bound to ask more than they could obtain."[47] The situation was very critical indeed. Sir Spencer Walpole summarized it well:

Three out of every four in Ireland would solve the problem by instituting a new university, endowed out of public funds and placed under exclusively Roman Catholic management. Three persons out of every four in Great Britain would turn out any Ministry which proposed to endow a Roman Catholic institution. There is no possible compromise between these opposite views. The conscience of the Nonconformists in England and of the Presbyterians in Scotland is opposed to the only remedy which the conscience of the Roman Catholics in Ireland will accept.[48]

---

[46] D. C. Lathbury (ed.), Correspondence on Church and Religion of William Ewart Gladstone (London: John Murray, 1910), II, p. 144.

[47] John Morley, op.cit., II, p. 437.

[48] Sir Spencer Walpole, The History of Twenty-five Years, 1856-1880 (London: Longmans, Green and Co., 1908), III, p. 260.

CHAPTER V

TOWARD REFORM IN HIGHER EDUCATION

After disestablishment, two important dicisions, expressed or understood, can be considered to have been made-- that university education should, bona fide, be equally accessible to all, and that the State ought not to endow denominational education. Reform in higher education was expected to proceed along these lines, but it was going to be a long and difficult path.

In his Bill of 1872, Mr. Fawcett proposed that Trinity College, the University and its Schools, as places of religion and learning, should be made accessible to all Her Majesty's subjects, by the abolition of all religious tests.[1] Mr. Fawcett proposal which included a Divinity School with a divinity professor who was not required to subscribe to any article of faith, or to profess any religion, implied the need for a separation of the theological faculties from rinity College and from the University. But the disestablished Church was not expected to have an exclusive theological faculty in a mixed university, nor was Parliament prepared to establish theological faculties for all sects. Such a dilemma provided fertile soil for Gladstone's own proposals.

As he stood on the verge of introducing the Irish University Bill of 1873, Gladstone seemed very much impressed with the need for higher education reform in Ireland. In his speech, he stressed the need for a revision of the constitution of Trinity College, as well as the improvement of the status of the University of Dublin as distinct from Trinity College. He also pointed to the limited number of those being educated in the arts: "I take the year 1871... Seven-hundred and eighty-four is the whole number of students who are receiving regular instruction in arts for the whole of Ireland, with its five million and a half of population."[2] In strong appeal

---

[1] Great Britain, 3 <u>Hansard's Parliamentary Debates</u>, 1872, CCX, p. 328.

[2] <u>Annual Register</u>, 1873, p. 12.

he then said, "I come now to the question of the practical principles on which we hope Parliament will conduct that great academical reform to which I have pointed by means of the measure we are about to introduce."[3] Gladstone summarized the bill as a step taken in the direction of abolition of tests, open endowments, and emancipation of the University from the Colleges. He had taken time to outline carefully the plans for the government, faculty, and finances of the proposed university.[4]

The principle of Gladstone's Irish University Bill of 1873 was along the lines recommended by William Monsell to Archbishop Cullen in 1869 at the time of disestablishment. The University of Dublin, separate from Trinity College, was to be converted into an Irish National University. As a federal institution with affiliated colleges, it would enjoy exclusive degree-granting privileges. The University was to be an examining body comprised of Trinity College, the Queen's Colleges of Belfast and Cork, the Catholic College of Maynooth, Magee College in Londonderry, and any other approved by Parliament, and the governing body. Nominally, the new University was to be considered a teaching body also, although theology, modern history, and moral philosophy which might be taught by the constituent colleges, were to be excluded from the curriculum. The imposition of all religious tests or religious qualifications for any purpose whatsoever was to cease. Funds from Trinity College and the State as well as what remained from endowments of the disestablished Church were to be used for the upkeep of the University.[5] In this way, Gladstone had hoped to find a solution to the university education problem in Ireland, but he was to be sorely disappointed.

For a short time only the bill seemed to have had a favorable reception. Justin McCarthy stated that "this scheme looked plausible and even satisfactory for a moment. It was met that first night with

---

[3]Ibid., p. 14.

[4]Ibid., p. 17ff.

[5]Great Britian, *Parliamentary Papers*, Vol. VI (1873), 329 for the full text of the provisions of the Irish University Bill of 1873.

something like a chorus of approval."[6] It was not long, however, before the most adverse reaction set in as Catholics and Anglicans alike, Nonconformist and Presbyterians denounced the bill. It was evident that this kind of reaction would follow even before the bill was introduced. Lord Kimberley made note of this in his journal, January 1, 1873: "Steer as we will the danger is great, as it appears to be absolutely impossible to reconcile the pretensions of our Nonconformist and Roman Catholic supporters."[7] This statement had foundation. On March 9, 1873, Cardinal Cullen issued a pastoral letter to all the Catholic churches condemning the measure. He spoke of the bill "as richly endowing non-Catholic and godless colleges, and without giving one farthing to Catholics, inviting them to compete in their poverty produced by penal laws and confiscations, with those left in possession of enormous wealth."[8]

Cardinal Cullen further lamented the inadequacy of the proposed university, pointing out that the plan, as outlined, increased the number of Queen's Colleges, and gave a new impulse to "that sort of teaching which separates education from religion."[9] The significance of that statement lay in the way it reflected the impact on education of the disestablishment principle of the separation of Church and State. After disestablishment, the State became more interested in education than in religion, as its long-standing united role in both religious and educational matters was disrupted. The State considered it its duty to provide education for each individual while religion was left to the churches. But Cardinal Cullen and the hierarchy had made it quite clear that they were not willing to abide by that principle, and their persistent desire to unite education and religion was a major difficulty in the settlement of the university question.

---

[6] Justin McCarthy, A History of Our Own Times (London: Chatts and Windus, 1880), IV, p. 389.

[7] Lord Kimberley, A Journal of Events During the Gladstone Ministry, 1868-1874, ed. Ethel Drus (London: Offices of the Royal Historical Society, 1958), p. 35.

[8] Patrick Moran, The Pastoral Letters and Other Writings of Cardinal Cullen (Dublin: Brown and Nolan, 1882), pp. 500-501.

[9] Ibid.

Disestablishment may therefore be said to have intensified the struggle between the secularists, generally represented by the Liberals on one hand, and the denominationalists, the Irish Catholic hierarchy, on the other.

The Irish Catholic hierarchy continued to oppose the Irish University Bill of 1873. In an interview with Cardinal Cullen on February 25, 1873, at Dublin Castle, Lord Spencer, Lord Lieutenant of Ireland, 1886-1874, discovered that Cardinal Cullen was quite hostile to the continuance of the Queen's Colleges, and the possible pertuantion of the mixed system of education. Cullen was also bitterly opposed to continued endowment of Trinity College, especially if the Catholic University still received no form of assistance or endowment. Cullen expressed to Spencer that the measure was the direct opposite of what the Catholics had hoped for, and that they would not be satisfied with anything less than guaranteed sums of money for redressing inequality and erecting new buildings.[10] The Catholic University strongly objected to the provision allowing for the affiliation of colleges in any part of Ireland to the new University of Dublin.

Not only the Catholic University, but Trinity College as well objected to the affiliation of colleges. The Catholic University, on the one hand, feared, as stated in its petition, that "very many parents would be tempted by various motives to keep their sons in provincial schools...and thus the Catholic University would, from want of students, be unable to compete with its richly endowed and numerously attended rivals, and so would soon practically cease to exist."[11] Trinity College, on the other hand, protested that "the standard of attainment necessary for an academical degree would be lowered by the affiliation of small provincial schools or colleges, inasmuch as the standard must necessarily be accommodated to the level of the more backward colleges."[12] These objections were prompted mainly by provisions in the Irish University Bill of 1873 which made it possible for students not enrolled in a college to take university degrees.

---

[10] John Morley, The Life of William Ewart Gladstone (New York: The MacMillan Company, 1911), II, p. 440.

[11] "The Irish University Bill," Saturday Review, XXXV (March, 1873), p. 264.

[12] Ibid.

The Presbyterians also objected to college affiliations. On February 24, 1873, the Resolutions of the Standing Committee (on Trinity College) of the General Assembly of the Irish Presbyterian Church, approved the separation of the theological faculty from the University of Dublin and from Trinity College as proposed in the bill. They also expressed the desire to see Trinity College open her doors, so that everyone of her Majesty's subjects regardless of creed or sect might benefit from its secular advantages. But the Resolutions were not without some objections:

> We object to the recognition by the State of denominational colleges, as part of a national system of University Education, and to the affilitation of such colleges with the University of Dublin. We object to the representation of denominational colleges as such on the council of the University of Dublin.[13]

Not withstanding adverse criticisms, Gladstone assured Queen Victoria of his continued faith in the Irish University Bill of 1873, the aim of which was, "to reform University Education in Ireland, for the removal of grievances and the advancement of learning."[14] Various groups condemned the same Bill for different reasons. Both the Roman Catholics who thought that the Bill had not gone far enough, and the Nonconformists who felt that it went too far, were angered at the proposal to endow denominational education. The Anglican Protestants resented the destruction of the historic University of Dublin. Men of learning and culture could not tolerate the idea of a national university without chairs in modern history and moral philosophy. The university, in their view, could not then be considered complete. Moreover, it was argued, that if these subjects were excluded from the university curriculum, the value of the Dublin honors would, as a result, be lower than those of the English universities. Vernon Harcourt, the Oxford Representative who had made known

---

[13] Great Britain, Parliamentary Papers, 1873, LII, 490, "Resolutions of the Standing Committee (on Trinity College) of the General Assembly of the Irish Presbyterian Church on the Subject of the Irish University Bill," p. 1.

[14] The Queen and Mr. Gladstone, ed. Philip Guedalla (New York: Doubleday, Loran and Co., Inc., 1934), Mr. Gladstone to Queen Victoria, February 1, 1873.

his intention to vote for the bill, declared against the clauses which prohibited the teaching of ethics and modern history as "the anathema of the Vatican against modern civilization."[15]

Consciousness of Vatican influence on the Catholic bishops had led Gladstone to make other compromises in the gagging clauses, i.e., those clauses relating to tests and the theological faculty. One of these clauses stated that "the council shall have power to question, reprimand or punish by suspension, deprivation or otherwise, any professor, teacher or examiner...who may by word of mouth, writing or otherwise, be held...to have given offence to the religious convictions of any member of the University."[16] This greatly upset young Liberals and Radicals who saw eye to eye with the Nonconformists and refused to support the bill, which they thought had reflected too strongly the Catholic objectives. The Radicals declared against what they considered "the humiliating precautions of the bill against proselytism, and the alleged inclination of the Government to conciliate the priesthood."[17]

But the Irish Catholic priesthood did not appreciate the efforts at conciliation and compromise that Gladstone had made. Through the Irish members, they sent a petition to Parliament denouncing anything in the bill that savored of mixed education, and criticizing the manner of the distribution of endowments. The Saturday Review noted that "the arguments used by the Roman Catholic members were merely amplifications of the resolutions adopted by the Irish Catholic bishops."[18] Gladstone quickly recognized the political power of the Irish Catholic hierarchy and its threat to the successful passage of the Irish University Bill. His report to the Queen on March 8, 1873 expressed great concern for the future of the Bill:

---

[15]Great Britain, 3 Hansard's Parliamentary Debates, CCXIV (1873), p. 1630.

[16]Great Britain, Parliamentary Papers, 1873, VI, 329, "A Bill for the Extension of University Education, Ireland," p. 4.

[17]Annual Register, 1873, p. 23.

[18]"The Irish University Debate," Saturday Review, XXXV (March, 1873), p. 302.

> Strange to say, it is the opposition of the
> Roman Catholic bishops that brings about the
> present difficulty...All these bishops,
> working upon liberal Irish members through
> their political interest in their seats, have
> proceeded so far that from twenty to twenty-
> five may go against the bill and as many may
> stay away. When to these are added the small
> knot of discontented Liberals and mere fanatics
> which so large a party commonly contains, the
> Government majority, now taken at 85 disappears.[19]

The political fortunes of the Irish University Bill of 1873 were further compounded by the opposition of the Conservative Party. During the second reading of the Bill in the Commons, the Conservative Leader, Benjamin Disraeli, attacked the already criticized provision for the removal of mental and moral philosophy and modern history from the curriculum of the proposed university. Disraeli declared that he must vote against a measure which he believed "to be monstrous in its general principles, pernicious in many of its details and utterly futile as a measure of practical legislation."[20] The Conservative party supported by the Irish Catholic members as well as some Radical and Nonconformist Liberals voted against the Irish University Bill; it was defeated by 287 votes to 284.[21] Curiously enough, while Cardinal Cullen, head of the Roman Catholic Church in Ireland, was bitterly opposed to the Bill, Cardinal Manning, head of the Roman Catholic Church in England, was favorably disposed to it. The Liberal Government was brought down, and Gladstone was quite upset by this frustration of his efforts. But perhaps he could find solace in the words of Manning, who wrote to him on March 12, 1873: "This is not your fault, nor the Bill's fault, but the fault of England and Scotland, and three anti-Catholic centuries."[22]

---

[19] John Morley, op.cit., II, 441.

[20] Annual Register, 1873, p. 29.

[21] Great Britain, 3 Hansard's Parliamentary Debates, CCXIV 1873, p. 1863.

[22] John Morley, The Life of William Ewart Gladstone, Vol. II, p. 440.

For the most part, the avenue through which the evils of three anti-Catholic centuries had perpetrated themselves was the Irish Anglican Establishment. It had affected Irish Catholic society at all points including education which the Catholics were particularly concerned about. Gladstone had brought about disestablishment. The Catholics had given him full support in this with an eye to a solution of the university question. But how disappointing it must have been for Gladstone to realize that he was forsaken by the Catholics after such a courtship with them at the time of disestablishment!

To the bishops, the correction of educational grievances was of supreme importance, and while disestablishment was a significant step in that direction, the Catholics looked beyond this to more direct actions. Disestablishment to the Catholics was not the complete answer to the educational problem, and Gladstone himself was soon aware that, contrary to expectations, it had not been as successful to his Irish policy as he had hoped. His stern realization of the prime importance of the university question was revealed in two questions he asked during his very able defence of the Irish University Bill: "What is to be the policy that is to follow the rejection of the Bill?" and "What is to be the policy adopted in Ireland?"[23]

Gladstone's policy of remedying the wrongs in Irish higher education was defeated. But while the Irish University Bill was a failure from a party point of view, the significance of the step which was taken to solve the university education problem in Ireland must not be overlooked. Within one week after reluctantly returning to office, the Prime Minister sought to inspire hope for the future, as he spoke at a Lord Mayor's dinner:

> We fell in the attempt to emancipate a great historic university in a sister country... and we had sought to make that university the proud and noble inheritance of every son of Ireland, without the smallest reference to his politics, to his party, or to his religious persuasion. Though we may have suffered in that enterprise, I believe, my Lord, that the

---

[23] Annual Register, 1873, p. 32.

> prinicple upon which we have proceeded is
> indestructible, and will yet make itself
> felt in the history of this country.[24]

The principle to which Gladstone referred here embodied the formation of a National University comprised of affiliated colleges. This was eventually achieved in 1908, and it is not difficult to see that the Irish University Bill of 1873 had acted as the springboard for the subsequent steps that were taken to attain that goal.

After 1873, the first step toward the final settlement of the university question in Ireland was the passage of the Irish University Bill of 1879 by the Conservatives. That Bill was approved to a large degree by the Catholics who insisted that their students should mix almost completely with others of their own faith while getting a university education. This was made possible by the Bill's proposals to endow the affiliated colleges, providing not only for the payment of their heads or governing bodies, and lecturers, but also for "the erection, establishment and maintenance of... museums, libraries and laboratories."[25] There was little doubt that the majority of endowed colleges were Roman Catholic. It will be remembered that the problem of concurrent endowment of educational institutions was a major issue at the time of disestablishment, and that it had an adverse effect on the Irish University Bill of the Liberals in 1873. The Conservatives had thus scored a victory by avoiding the stand the Liberals had taken against denominationally endowed colleges. Gladstone's experience had therefore provided valuable lessons for Disraeli and the Conservatives.

In a more positive way, however, Gladstone's Irish University Bill of 1873 contributed to the university settlement of 1879. State supervision of the teaching of secular subjects at the Roman Catholic colleges as well as the State's entire management and superintendence over the affairs, concerns, and property of the said university, were features of the abortive Irish University Bill of 1873 which were adopted by the Irish University Act of 1879. So close was the resemblance between them, that the Saturday Review noted that the

---

[24]"The Irish University Bill and the Defeat of the Ministry," *Quarterly Review*, CXXXIV, 1873, p. 552.

[25]Great Britain, *Parliamentary Papers*, 1879, VII (577), "A Bill to Make Better Provision for University Education in Ireland," p. 3.

Act of 1879 was "exactly on a footing with Mr. Gladstone's unfortunate measure."[26] It is worthy of note, too, that the Irish Church Act of 1869 had influenced the agreement reached on higher education in 1879. Clause 21 of the Irish University Act of 1879 provided that "the several provisions of the Irish Church Act, 1869, with respect to the raising of money by the Commissioners of Church Temporalities in Ireland...shall be extended and shall apply to the purposes of this Act..."[27]

Consequent to the Irish University Act of 1879, the Royal University of Ireland was chartered. Incorporated in 1880, it was empowered to grant degrees (except in medicine) to all those who had passed the examinations which its senate prescribed, whether they had studied at a university college or not. But neither this nor indeed Disraeli's compromise, could satisfy those who stood on either side of denominational education, and this led to finding new avenues for the solution of the university question in Ireland.

One of the alternative schemes for a settlement of the university question in 1890 by William Walsh, Roman Catholic Archbishop of Dublin (1885-1921), and which was accepted by the Catholics, was "one state-recognized university embracing all colleges fulfilling certain educational conditions (the Gladstone plan)."[28] Up to this time, therefore, the Catholics still saw wisdom in Gladstone's scheme. The next two decades were to see fast breaking efforts stemming from the chain of actions and reactions associated not only with the Irish University Bill of 1873, but also with the Irish Church disestablishment of 1869.

Following disestablishment, perhaps the biggest problem for the Catholics, was acceptance of the principle that the State must not in future create or endow any denominational institution in Ireland. This principle seemed to have been finally established by Gladstone's Irish Church Act of 1869, which put an end to all connection between the State and the churches, including the annual grants to Maynooth College and to the Presbyterian Church. Negotiations between the

---

[26]"The Irish University Bill," *Saturday Review*, XLVII, May, 1879. p. 603.

[27]Great Britain, *Parliamentary Papers*, 1879, VII, "A Bill to Make Better Provision for University Education in Ireland," p. 5.

[28]T. W. Moody, "The Irish University Question of the Nineteenth Century," in *History*, XLIII 1958, p. 103.

Catholic hierarchy and the government only served to intensify
Protestant, Nonconformist, and Presbyterian support of the non-
sectarian principle, and of the mixed system of education as represented by the Queen's University system. But the Catholics would
not be reconciled. They were dissatisfied with the Royal University of 1880 because it conformed to the nonsectarian principle.
Moreover, the funds provided by Parliament for university buildings for that university, and the ₤20,000 a year for exhibitions,
scholarship, and fellowships were aiding secular education to
which the Catholics objected.

In fact, the Royal University scheme differed fundamentally
from its predecessors in that provision was made for the indirect
endowment of the Catholic University. The statutes of the Royal
University, which received confirmation by the Crown in 1881,
authorized the senate to select not more than twenty-nine university fellows to teach matriculated students at an approved educational institution. The fellows who were to conduct university
examinations would receive a salary of ₤400 per annum.[29] The
senate decided to assign half the fellowships to professors in the
arts faculty of the Catholic University (called University College,
Dublin, after 1882), and the remainder to the Queen's Colleges at
Belfast, Galway, and Cork, and to Magee College in Londonderry. By
this means, the Catholic University received an endowment of ₤6,000
per year, thus setting aside though not openly, the principle
that public money must not be used to subsidize sectarian institutions. Gradually there was yielding to the pressure for the endowment of a separate Catholic institution. That pressure had become
intensified since disestablishment, when men like Isaac Butt pleaded
such a cause.

In 1875, Isaac Butt wrote a stirring pamphlet entitled "The
Problem of Irish Education." In it he emphasized the need for endowing a Catholic University:

> There ought to be provided for this (Catholic)
> College an endowment substantially equal to that
> enjoyed by Trinity College. This should be made
> up of any money or property which the founders

---

[29]T. W. Moody, "The Irish University Question," in <u>History</u>,
Vol. XLIII, No. 148, 1958, p. 102.

of the College would bring with them, of a grant from the funds of Trinity College... and of a supplemental grant out of the surplus of the revenues of the disestablished Church.[30]

Other features of Gladstone's Irish University Bill of 1873 included provision for a tax on the funds of Trinity College for the proposed university; the tax which was not to exceed Ł12,000 per year, was commutable on payment of a lump sum of Ł300,000. That Bill also proposed that a portion of the surplus of Church property be used for erecting academic buildings for the university. Butt's idea, in addition, was that a separate amount be appropriated from the disestablished Church surplus revenues to academic buildings for the Catholic College.

Butt strongly defended his position with regard to Church surplus revenues. He said that he knew that many would be surprised at his reference to the Act of Church disestablishment--"an act which proceeded on the maxim that revenues devoted to the religious purposes of the whole people ought no longer to be applied for those of a small minority."[31] Butt further said that he knew that a general principle has been established in the Irish Church Act of 1869 which prohibited the maintenance of a University system of which religion forms a part."[32] Butt then explained that the principle had failed as the very men who urged the argument were preparing to maintain in the reformed Trinity College at least two forms of worship. Moreover, even Gladstone's Church Act left Trinity College free to provide any religious instruction the authorities thought fit, provided such was not forced on the student. Indeed, the Irish Church Act that disestablished the Church was not intended to make the people less religious. It was assumed that the Irish people would have the same ecclesiastical establishments that they had before, and naturally, that they would put up claims for their own educational institutions. The endowment of these institutions was a cardinal factor to the Catholics in the struggle for higher education reform.

---

[30]Isaac Butt, *The Problem of Irish Education, an Attempt at Its Solution* (London: Longmans, Green and Co., 1875), p. 53.

[31]Ibid., p. 100.

[32]Ibid.

Butt's arguments for endowment supported the Catholic case. He insisted that disestablishment and disendowment are very significant for higher education reform. He pointed out that the surplus of the Church property was essentially and purely an Irish one, and that it was the English who had squandered away the vast wealth of the Church leaving only a small surplus of five million pounds. His remarks on the need for redress are important:

> Is nothing due to the Catholic people of Ireland, whom English power so long deprived of all benefit from these endowments? Will the granting of the poor pittance be anything like reparation for that gigantic wrong? Will not its refusal be the perpetuation of the very spirit of intolerance and injustice which prompted the infliction of the wrong?...Will it teach Ireland to see in the act of disestablishment any real desire to redress?[33]

Butt had rightly shown that the endowment of a Catholic College was one of the chief ways in which the English Government could convince the Irish Catholics that it had really abandoned the policy which had so long tried to suppress their religion, a policy which it outlawed by the Act for disestablishment. Whether or not these arguments had any direct effect on the decisions of the Conservative Government concerning the establishment of the Royal University, they are of consequence as a reflection of Catholic mood and agitation. They are of consequence, also, for their indirect effect on Conservative attitude toward higher education reform.

As Isaac Butt led the Liberal in the drive for Home Rule, he was fully aware that their effort could be undermined by the lack of interest long evident in the attitude of the Catholic bishops. However, Butt's concern for the education question appealed to the Catholics and sparked new interest in Home Rule. Moreover, as the Home Rulers declared for denominational education, they eventually secured the support of the Catholic priests who might have been earlier influenced by Catholic bishops with only minimal interest in Home Rule.

---

[33]*Ibid.*, p. 99.

declared for denominational education they secured the adhesion of the Catholic clergy, for the education question was of prime importance to them. The priests took a big part in the 1874 election which brought the Conservatives, led by Disraeli, to power, and it was under Conservative Government that the Royal University was established.

The implicit endowment of the Catholic College of the Royal University, although not recognized by the Catholics themselves nor indeed by anyone, was a great boon to the College. The fellowship system rescued the College from a desperate situation, placing it on a new path to become the rival of the Queen's Colleges for the rewards of the Royal University. It quickly earned a high reputation for both the quality of its teaching and the prowess of its students. In fact, students from the Queen's Colleges soon complained that in the university examinations they were hardly able to compete with those of the Catholic University. Some patrons had tried to save the Queen's University not only because of its high quality education, but also because of its non-sectarian character. The situation in 1874 was different from what it was in 1873, for the Catholics as a body supported Disraeli's scheme, and Trinity College was not opposed to it. Gladstone, faced with the decision to annul or carry out the scheme, realized the danger of rejecting such a recent parliamentary decision.

In 1882, the Queen's University was dissolved. The Queen's Colleges were no longer the constituent colleges of a teaching university, but rather they became colleges of indeterminate status, loosely connected with a university that was merely an examining body. This change saw a shift in Catholic preponderance. On the senate of the Queen's University, the presidents of the colleges. On the senate of the Royal University, the presidents and other representatives of the colleges were well outnumbered by members who represented other, and more particularly Catholic, interests.

Although Catholics admitted that the Royal University of 1880 was a considerable improvement on the Queen's University, they considered that it was still far from what they desired. Even Protestants viewed it as a temporary solution. Catholics continued to demand that there must be public endowment for a Catholic college in Dublin, with status and advantages equal to that of Trinity College. Since disestablishment, the Catholics had been watching developments at Trinity College or the University of Dublin, and whatever changes took place in the realm of Catholic education was weighed carefully in the light of such developments.

As long as Ireland possessed a national Church, it was the privilege and duty of Trinity College to devote its resources largely to the work of that Church. The Irish Church Act of 1869 which deprived the Church of its national position, forced Trinity to choose either to become a denominational seminary, having its endowments dealt with as national property, or to claim as one of the consequences of that Act, the right to devote itself directly and exclusively to national work. The Edinburgh Review noted in 1873 that immediately after the passage of the Irish Church Act of 1869 Trinity College claimed its right to carry on its work as a national institution.[34] That claim was rejected by the Ultramontanes.

The Ultramontane Party, i.e. the extreme conservative wing of the Catholic hierarchy refused to accept Trinity College as a national institution on the basis of Cardinal Cullen's insistence that "the nationality of Ireland means simply the Catholic Church."[35] The sequence of events therefore followed on the principle that Catholics would continue to press for an institution to meet their needs. The Catholic hierarchy showed very little interest in the opening up of Trinity College. It was held by many leading Catholics that Fawcett's proposals to abolish tests and thereby open up Trinity College would not help the situation very much, but would only add a fourth mixed college which would be dreaded as much or even more than those already existing. The Catholics were not particularly interested in reform of the three Queen's Colleges at Galway, Belfast and Cork except on their own terms. Hence Disraeli's decision in 1879 to leave these colleges as well as Trinity College untouched was not opposed by them for the time being.

During the whole of Cullen's time-- that is for about thirty years after the controversy about university education in Ireland had become acute by reason of the establishment of the Queen's Colleges-- the Catholic demand was for a Catholic University rather than for reform of Trinity College or the Queen's Colleges. This was to be a university or college in which the Canon Law of the Catholic Church would rule, so that no one would be admitted to office or continue to hold it except in accor-

---

[34]"The Ministry and University Education in Ireland," *Edinburgh Review*, Vol. 134, 1873, p. 256.

[35]*Ibid.*, p. 257.

dance with the Canons. This was the Catholic demand as late as 1885. In their Resolutions of that year, the bishops stated that their demands "would be satisfied substantially by the establishment... of one or more Colleges conducted on purely Catholic principles."[36]

The end of the Cullen era, however, saw the signs of modification in these demands. Cullen died in 1878, and after his death the trend was still for a separate Catholic institution, but on less stringent terms. The fact that the Catholics did accept the Royal University even though only partially, was evident of a slight change in attitude. Toward the end of the nineteenth century, the various proposals for reform could be reduced to two classes: (1) the remodelling of Trinity College and the Queen's Colleges so as to make them acceptable to Catholics, and (2) the establishment in Dublin, with University College (i.e., the former Catholic University) and the Catholic University School of Medicine as nuclei, of a new college that might be Catholic in the sense that Trinity College was Protestant. The emphasis seemed to be more on a college for Catholics than on a Catholic college, and that is a very important distinction. This was to be the guiding motive for the university settlement in 1908.

A few years before the final solution of the Irish university education problem, the Catholic bishops indicated a departure from the earlier position adhered to in Cullen's time. In 1903, the Robertson Commission recommended that all offices in the new college for Catholics should be open to persons of all denominations, subject only to the condition that the holders should not teach or publish anything contrary to the doctrine of the Catholic Church. The observance of the condition in any given case was to be decided by a Board of Four Visitors-- two being Catholics, the other two being judges not necessarily Catholics. This was accepted more than once by the Catholic bishops, as was stated by the Standing Committee of the Archbishops and Bishops of Ireland, July 25, 1906.[37] In 1897, the hierarchy drew up a statement in which they declared, that "with some modifications in the Act (the Tests Act of 1873)...

---

[36]"The Catholic University Question," Catholic University Bulletin, Vol. XIV, 1908, p. 255.

[37]Ibid., p. 256.

we have no objection to the opening up of the degrees, honours and Emoluments to all comers."[38] The non-sectarian principle, which was an outgrowth of disestablishment and which had become a major issue, was at last acceded to.

An open endorsement of the non-sectarian principle by the Catholics was shown in 1907 when James Bryce, Chief Secretary for Ireland, announced his plan for a settlement of the university question. This plan called for the enlargment of the University of Dublin to include with Trinity College, the Queen's Colleges of Belfast, Cork, and a Catholic College in Dublin. This university was to be non-sectarian, and would provide alternative classes for Protestants and Catholics in controversial subjects: Queen's College at Galway, Maynooth College and Magee College, Londonderry, were to be associated with the university as affiliated institutions. The Catholics accepted this plan which was nothing but a revised version of Gladstone's. It took a little time for the seeds sown at the time of disestablishment to bear fruit. As the winds of strife died down, the principles enunciated then were gradually accepted with time. It is true that the Bryce plan was not implemented on account of staunch opposition from those Protestants who wished to see Trinity College remain untouched. The final scheme, which was based on Balfour's proposal in 1899, left Trinity College unmolested, but also incorporated some of the features of Bryce's plan.

By the final university settlement in 1908, two new universities were created-- one centered at Dublin for Catholics, and the other at Belfast for Protestants. Both were free from religious tests, and neither could use public endowment for religious purposes. The Queen's Colleges of Cork and Galway were to be constituent colleges of the university based at Dublin, and Maynooth was to be a recognized college. The endowment problem was a compromise on the part of the State, just as concession to the non-sectarian principle was a compromise on the part of Catholics. The two universities, the Queen's University at Belfast, and the National University at Dublin, were endowed with an annual income from the State, no part of which might be used to maintain places of worship or religious teaching. On the whole, British policy on the university question initiated in 1845 and

---

[38]Ibid., p. 257.

reinforced at the time of disestablishment, had endeavored to follow the theory that the State ought not to endow denominational education.

In practice, however, the theory of non-endowment for religious education did not hold very well. The National University of Ireland, without being a Catholic University was intended to be a university designed to meet the needs and expectations of Catholics and everyone else. The university received an endowment of ₤74,000 a year from the State. This settlement has been considered a compromise, which, as Isaac Butt pointed out, was a step in the right direction, in the light of the implications of disestablishment.

Butt had shown that the Act for disestablishment did not necessarily prohibit the endowment of religious education:

> It does indeed lead us to the conclusion that no one religious persuasion has any exclusive right to these endowments, but it carries us no further. We absolutely refuse to follow in our University legislation the precedent of the Church Act. By the provisions of the Church Act we have no endowed Church. If the analogy is really to guide us the inference is that we should have no endowed University.[39]

But Trinity College had remained well endowed and with its predominantly Protestant character. In 1882, The Month observed that "the Protestantism of the disestablished Church was in possession at Trinity College, and appeared even for special reasons likely to preserve its advantage."[40] The Protestant religion was still taught there as it had been in the past, and Protestant worship was still carried on. While Catholicism had by this time ceased to be a disability, it was still unable to gain equal footing and equal privileges with the disestablished creed. This was continuously a sore factor for Catholics, and they continued to press for their own institution.

---

[39] Isaac Butt, op.cit., p. 101.

[40] "The Progress of the Irish University Question," The Month, Vol. XLVI, 1882, p. 65.

When Trinity College opened up her doors after religious tests were abolished in 1873, the most that was held out to Catholics was competition in secular education which they despised. In addition to all this, the Catholics had kept a careful eye on the continued rich endowments of Trinity College. Up to 1980, as The Month noted, "the total endowments of Protestant and godless education in Ireland amounted to over 65,000 pounds."[41] The Month also pointed out that "the endowments of Catholic education are absolutely nothing, unless we reckon as an endowment the obligation of some dozen fellows or Teaching Examiners of the Royal University, to add to their duties as examiners, the duty of lecturing in the Catholic University of Dublin."[42]

On the question of endowments, The Month further claimed that inasmuch as the Catholics of Ireland outnumbered the Protestants four to one, "the endowments of Catholic education in Ireland, ought to be, as compared with the endowments of Protestant education, if perfect equality is to be maintained, at least as four to one."[43] In 1885, the Dublin Review insisted that Catholics of Ireland had the full right to "an endowment adequate to their wants and in the same proportion with their numbers as the endowments at present enjoyed by the non-catholic population of the country."[44] The three equalities of endowment, equipment, and prestige demanded by the Catholics vigorously since disestablishment had not been completely met by the establishment of the Royal University in 1880, although what was accomplished then was a very important step toward the final solution in 1908.

Meanwhile, other important changes had been effected in all branches of education in Ireland. The National School Teachers (Ireland) Act of 1875 made provision for the schools to earn grants for the teachers. In 1878, an Intermediate Education Board was set

---

[41] "University Education in Ireland," The Month, Vol. LXVIII, 1890, p. 24.

[42] Ibid.

[43] Ibid.

[44] "The Catholic Education Question in England and Ireland," Dublin Review, Vol. XIII, 1885, p. 189.

up in Dublin. Maynooth College became a constituent college of the Catholic University in 1876, and a University College in 1882; it was given over to the Jesuits in 1883. The National School Teachers' Residences Act of 1875 facilitated the erection of residences for teachers. The movement for compulsory education was also in progress in the late 1870's. In 1883, a motion was agreed to in the House of Commons on the principle of compulsory education in Ireland as far as "the social and religious conditions of the country required."[45]

The disestablishment and disendowment of the Irish Church provided the basis for some types of educational legislation, not the least of which was the Teachers' Act of 1879. That Act initiated a fund for teachers' pensions by setting aside a sum of £1,300,000 from the property of the disestablished Church. The Irish University Act of 1876, the Bill to amend the laws relating to the Queen's Colleges and the Queen's University in Ireland in 1878, and the University Education (Ireland) Act, 1878-79, indicate efforts that were made to improve higher education in Ireland.

---

[45]Great Britain, 3 Hansard's Parliamentary Debates, CCLXXVI, p. 1299.

CHAPTER VI

REVIEW AND ASSESSMENT

The disestablishment of the Irish Church in 1869 had a twofold effect upon the university question in Ireland during the decade which followed. In some respects, it somewhat smoothed the way for a settlement and in other respects it complicated the problem. It is necessary to look at both sides in evaluating the impact of disestablishment on the higher education problem in Ireland. The Church disestablishment involved the dissolution of a great corporation, very widely extended, and of powerful influence. The Land Act of 1870 required even more than the destruction of a great corporate body; it embodied the modification, to some extent, of long-established individual vested rights. The educational demands of Catholic Ireland were only indirectly related to the effectiveness of the Irish Church Act of 1869, and the Irish Land Act of 1870. Such effectiveness, which was aimed at Protestancy ascendancy, was indispensable to Catholic aspirations in the struggle for educational equality.

Catholics were bitterly opposed to the Irish Anglican Establishment in general, because it upheld the privileges of the Protestant minority in every aspect of society including education. They were especially bitter over conscious efforts of the Establishment to suppress Catholicism through educational means. Cardinal Cullen, in his Pastoral letter for the festival of St. Patrick, in 1871, directed against the Irish Establishment, charged that other "means having also been found insufficient, the enemies of Catholicity concentrated all their forces upon education."[1]

Henceforth, the desire to defend, uphold, and enhance Catholicism at the expense of Protestantism would be foremost in the minds of the hierarchy, even if things were improving somewhat after disestablishment. For while it cannot be denied that the Establishment was an obstacle and a burden to Catholics, it was not nearly as bad as it might have

---

[1] P. F. Moran, The Pastoral Letter and Other Writings of Cardinal Cullen (Dublin: Browne and Nolan, 1882), III, p. 499.

been before the 1830's. The Temporalities Act of 1833 had abolished the cess or the exaction of provisions at a fixed price for the supply of the household and soldiers of the Lord Lieutenant of Ireland. Five years later, the tithe was converted into a rent-charge which was payable by the owners of land who were largely Protestants, and not by the tenants, who were mainly Catholics. In fact as a result of these statutory changes restricting Protestant privileges, the Irish Catholic bishops did not consider it necessary to renew their agitation against the abuses of the Establishment until 1864.

The Catholic bishops became alarmed with the Protestant Revival in 1859, and swiftly condemned it. Their fears were multiplied by the Government's proposal in the same year for a system of mixed intermediate education. From 1859 they engaged in a sequence of political agitation until 1873 when they helped bring about the fall of the Gladstone Ministry. The bishops had given Gladstone their support up to that time, but perhaps Gladstone had misunderstood it, for they were less interested in political questions than in religious and educational questions. To the bishops, the education question was not at all political: it was at the heart of a network of proselytism and indifferentism which they regarded as the outstanding characteristic of the Protestant Constitution. Hence, their interest in disestablishment went beyond political or even civil considerations, as the bishops looked to the effect that it would have on Catholic education.

Irish Catholics were always concerned about the adverse impact of Protestant ascendancy on their educational system. Cardinal Cullen referred to that concern as he addressed the literary and historical society of the Catholic University in 1869:

> But it is not my intention to treat about the Church Bill...I shall rather call your attention to the effects which that spirit of ascendancy, which shall soon be banished from the country, has produced on Catholic education in Ireland during the last three centuries.[2]

---

[2] P. F. Moran, op.cit., Vol. III, p. 226.

The Cullen era was to be marked by definite aspirations for
the future of Catholic education following disestablishment, as the
Cardinal further pointed out in his reference to the Irish Church Bill:

> ...It may be, indeed, that the House of Lords
> will not listen to the voice of the country,
> and that the Church Bill...will be mutilated
> in the Upper House...; but still, it cannot be
> denied that a great blow has been struck at the
> foundations of intolerance and exclusiveness,
> and that the whole fabric of ascendancy is
> reduced to such a tottering state that, even
> if disappointed this year, our wishes must be
> satisfied in a short time.[3]

The remarks of the Cardinal also revealed the determination of the
hierarchy to press for claims beyond what was expressed or even
implied by the Church Act:

> We may add that, perhaps a little delay will
> bring us a fuller measure of justice than the
> higher branch of the legislature is disposed to
> grant us at present.[4]

Perhaps, one way in which the Catholics followed up this determination
was through their insistence--against the wishes of Gladstone and the Liberals--that Maynooth should be treated as an educational rather than an
ecclesiastical endowment. They did this to circumvent the principle
of non-endowment of religious education which the Church Act implied.
But Gladstone was not as fully cognizant of all this as he should have
been. He told Fortescue in 1870 that on the question of university
education the Government knew what it would give the Catholics whether
they would take it or not. Gladstone also communicated his intention
in a letter to the President of Maynooth in 1873: "I think if upon the
whole, we are met in the same spirit as in 1869 and 1870, we may, please
God, accomplish this step also towards the improvement of Ireland."[5]

---

[3] Ibid., p. 225.

[4] Ibid.

[5] Correspondence on Church and Religion of W. E. Gladstone,
edited by D. C. Lathbury (London: John Murray, 1910), II, p. 144.

Gladstone was too optimistic in his attempt to settle the university question in 1873 in the same spirit as in 1869 and 1870". The university problem, although in some ways related to the Church and land questions was essentially different. The Quarterly Review pointed very poignantly to the fact that the history and position of Trinity College or the University of Dublin, as a public institution, distinguished it from the Church. Although it was founded by the State, it was not under State control; it had a life of its own apart from the Government, a fact which was recognized by the Irish people. Assailants of the Irish Church avoided treating Trinity College as an appendage of the Church. The influences that had hampered the work of the Church, and confused the relations of landlord and tenant had not materially affected the career of the University of Dublin.[6] It was not going to be easy to apply to the University of Dublin exactly the same process that had been applied to the Church Establishment, i.e., to disestablish education and devote the funds obtained through disendowment to welfare work in Ireland. Again, the disestablishment process was influenced, on the one hand, by the principle of State non-recognition of religion, and on the other, by the tendency toward a greater role of the State in education. This latter was one of the principal features of the Enlightenment.

Catholic acceptance or rejection of Enlightenment ideas was crucial to the success or failure of the efforts to solve the university question. In general, it may be said that the Catholics defended the ideas of the Enlightenment at this time. Cardinal Cullen, in an assessment of the Irish Church Bill of 1869 admitted that it was prepared by the most liberal and enlightened Statesman of the day. He also charged Protestantism and the Establishment for stifling educational progress:

> If education is not as advanced as it ought to be amongst the majority of the people of Ireland, the fault is not to be attributed to any want of love of learning, or of exertions to promote it on their part, but to the despotism with which the votaries of the dominant faction crushed every attempt that was made to promote enlightenment.[7]

---

[6]"The Ministry and University Education in Ireland," Quarterly Review, Vol. CXXXIV, 1873, pp. 258-259.

[7]P. F. Moran, op.cit., III, p. 144.

Other aspects of Enlightenment were less appealing to the Catholics. For instance, when the principle of non-endowment of religious education by the State was enunciated following disestablishment, they were not very happy. They were strongly opposed to all forms of secular or united education which was endorsed by the State, and they welcomed State aid for religious education, which was the very opposite of what the Enlightenment stood for.

The inconsistency of the Catholic attitude toward the Enlightenment was not unmatched by the inconsistency of the Government's policy in England and in Ireland. Even though Parliament had aided schools through denominational grants in England, it feared the possibility of "endowing error" in Ireland except in the case of Maynooth. Of course, the Catholic bishops protested the Government's policy toward Ireland and made demands for the adoption of the English method or State denominational endowment of education. The Endowed Schools Act of 1869 in England barely showed tendencies toward secularism. At the same time, this was not very heartening to the bishops who were witnessing the passage of the Irish Church Act which confirmed the principle of no State assistance to religious education. The bishops seemed further perplexed and discouraged as they perceived additional signs of liberalism in Gladstone which were not in their interest. Cardinal Cullen wrote to Cardinal Manning early in 1873: "It is reported that Mr. Gladstone intends giving professorships to distinguished Germans and Frenchmen who will bring Hegelism and infidelity with them."[8]

Gladstone himself admitted that he was a liberal. In some autobiographical fragments written in 1892 under the heading "My Earlier Political Opinions," he stated, "I do not hesitate to say Oxford had... laid the foundation of my Liberalism."[9] His efforts to solve the Church, land, and university questions in Ireland indicated his liberal leanings. Prior to the passage of the Irish Church Act of 1869, talk about justice and equality for Ireland was not followed up with action and, consequently, the benefits of the Irish Anglican Church continued to outweigh those of the others. However, those extra benefits and privileges hitherto enjoyed by the Irish Anglican Church were curtailed by disestablishment, which became effective after the first day of January, 1871.

---

[8] "Irish Pages from the Postbags of Manning, Cullen and Gladstone," ed. Leslie Shane, Dublin Review, Vol. 165, 1919, p. 186.

[9] W. E. Gladstone, The Gladstone Papers (London: Cassell and Co., Limited, 1930), p. 95.

The democratic principle which affected the privileges of the Irish Anglican hierarchy also signalled a new day for the Irish Catholic Laity. Henceforth, as W. Maziere Brady pointed out, the laity as well as the bishops and clergy had "a voice in the appointment of the representative body to which, when incorporated, will belong all the property of the future Church, including the fabrics of places of worship, glebe houses and glebes."[10]

The democratic principle was also evident in the Land Act of 1870. The bulk of land was in the hands of Protestants who possessed absolute ownership, and this created a problem which adversely affected the university education question for a long time. With reference to Trinity College Cardinal Cullen insisted that: "the site on which this Protestant University was erected was Catholic religious property, confiscated in the reign of Henry VIII" and that "it was rapidly enriched with Catholic lands, till it became possessed of the property of about 200,000 acres, which it now holds."[11]

Gladstone was fully aware of the problem of land ownership. He had seen the keen interest of the bishops in that issue, and he also knew how dear to their heart was the education question. The Land Act of 1870, while not producing the desired effect, had set a very important precedent. Moreover, it legalized the Ulster Tenant Right and recognized that not only the owner, but also the occupier of the soil had a right in the land. Philip Magnus correctly observed that the Land Act of 1870 "established the far-reaching principle that property in land is not absolute."[12] That principle was an expression of Gladstonian liberalism.

It is evident that Gladstone intended to extend his liberal principle to the Irish University Bill of 1873. The proposed university was to be open. There were to be no religious tests for the university and anyone could take the examinations without attending the colleges. The Senate would consist of all graduates starting with those of Trinity College and the Queen's University; special powers up to 1878 were provided for admitting to the Senate persons from other colleges. In this way, Catholics could join the Senate from the beginning. But the bill failed.

---

[10] W. Maziere Brady, "Prospects of the Disestablished Church in Ireland," *Contemporary Review*, XII (Sept. - Dec., 1869), p. 12.

[11] P. F. Moran, op.cit., III, p. 229.

[12] Philip Magnus, *Gladstone: A Biography* (London: John Murray, 1954), p. 203.

The failure of the Irish University Bill of 1873 opened the door for Mr. Fawcett's modest proposal to abolish tests at Trinity College. Through his proposal, Fawcett gave a stimulus to Trinity College and to mixed education by enabling the university to open its prizes to students of every denomination. On the other hand he had perpetuated the grievance of which the Catholics complained before, that no means were available for the higher education of the members of their Church who objected to the association of their sons with men of another faith. Thus Fawcett had forced on Ireland an arrangement which Protestants and Liberals in Great Britain approved, but which the Catholics in Ireland disliked and condemned.

Without doubt, Irish Catholics also disliked and condemned anything in university reform which still carried the lingering effects of Protestant ascendancy. The diminution of that ascendancy was one of the main benefits they looked for in disestablishment, and they expected that university reform as an adjunct of disestablishment would be along similar lines. Accordingly, Cardinal Cullen made the following charge against the Irish University Bill of 1873 in a letter to Cardinal Manning on February 25, 1873:

> I cannot see how we can in anyway co-operate in carrying out the proposed measure... In the first place mixed education, or education without religion is directly sanctioned by the establishment of a Queen's College in Dublin, to be called Trinity College. This institution will have the immense buildings of the present Trinity College, with its libraries and museums, all of which or nearly all, are public property, and besides, 50,000 pounds per annum.[13]

To the Catholic hierarchy therefore, the Irish University Bill of 1873, seemed to be one way of perpetuating Protestant ascendancy. While they admitted that Catholic students would have some advantage under the plan by being able to obtain degrees without attending the university, they would have only small benefits, for their college being poor, only a few would have the means to prepare for the examinations. In his letter to Manning, Cullen further stated:

---

[13] Leslie Shane, "Irish Pages from the Postbags of Manning, Cullen and Gladstone," Dublin Review, Vol. 165, 1919, p. 186.

Mr. Gladstone in his speech, says that any of the present professors of Trinity College, who cannot be provided for in the new mixed college, may be appointed to chairs in the new University. In this way an ascendancy for Protestant teaching will be secured for the future.[14]

The Catholics were only too aware of the close association between the Church Establishment and Protestant higher education in Ireland. They must have taken careful note of men like James Whiteside, who threw their full weight behind the Irish Establishment. James Whiteside, who was champion of the Irish Establishment, was also the member of Parliament for the University of Dublin or Trinity College. In 1866, in a speech in the Commons, he showed how from time to time respect for the Irish Establishment was affirmed not only by bishops and archbishops of the Roman Catholic Church in Ireland, but also by professors at Maynooth College.[15]

In his defence of both the Irish Church Establishment and Protestant higher education, Whiteside expressed the symbol of oneness between them. Arguing for the retention of the Establishment he said, "I further feel that the Establishment in Ireland is the very cement of the Union. I find it interwoven with all the essential relations and institutions of the two kingdoms."[16] In this matter, what could be more important than his reference to educational institutions? A little earlier he had argued with equal force against any alteration in the Queen's University to meet Catholic demands.[17] In view of all this therefore, the Irish Catholics were bound to be very hesitant in their acceptance of anything in university reform which gave the slightest evidence of a continued Protestant ascendancy.

---

[14] Ibid.

[15] Great Britain, 3 Hansard's Parliamentary Debates, CLXXXII, (1866), p. 1053-54.

[16] Ibid., p. 1051.

[17] Ibid., CLXXX, p. 560.

They were not going to be very happy if the aims and objectives which they hoped would be strengthened by disestablishment were frustrated in any way by changes in the system of higher education.

Nor were the members of the Protestant Church very happy over certain things affecting Trinity College following disestablishment. They, too, felt entirely within their rights in frowning upon any scheme that was put forward if it infringed in any way upon their privileges. In the days before disestablishment all the Fellows at Trinity College (except two or three) were required to be in Holy Orders, and because of the valuable benefices in the patronage of the College, many of them were able to retire from academic life and devote their energies to pastoral work. Furthermore, the Crown had always looked to the clerical Fellows of Trinity College whenever there were vacant bishoprics to be filled. But, as the Church Quarterly Review stated, " all this has been swept away by Disestablishment and by the abolition of tests which was brought about by Fawcett's Act."[18] Only about four Fellows took Holy Orders in almost forty years after disestablishment. As a consequence, promotion was less rapid within Trinity College than it used to be. The change had "thus been silently brought about by Disestablishment and its consequences in the constitution of the Governing body."[19]

Another aspect of disestablishment which was of great concern to Protestants was the principle that the State should not endow denominational education. But this was a very deceptive principle, for, while at the time of disestablishment Maynooth College--the principal theological seminary of the Roman priesthood in Ireland--lost its annual grant, it was endowed in perpetuity by the payment from the public funds of a sum equal to fourteen times the amount it received annually from Parliament, i.e. a capital sum of approximately £400,000. Moreover, as the nineteenth century drew to a close, the majority of primary schools in Ireland fell more and more under Roman Catholic management and control; they were denominational in fact, even though not in name, and yet the cost of their maintenance was borne by the State. Again, the indirect endowment of University College, Dublin--a Jesuit institution--through funds received from

---

[18] "Irish University Education and the Reform of Trinity College, Dublin," Church Quarterly Review, Vol. LXIII, 1906, p. 168.

[19] Ibid.

the Royal University for the appointment of Jesuit Fathers as examiners and Fellows in that institution could hardly be thought of as anything else but the endowment of denominational education. Such provisions were regarded by Protestant critics as most offensive, and it is not difficult to see why they became upset over any tendency to endow religious education. After all, they could perceive that the secularizing principle would in time strongly affect Trinity College especially as that principle was a prime factor in disestablishment.

At the time of disestablishment, the Irish Catholic bishops adhered to their Resolutions of 1867 declaring that they upheld the principle of secularization of ecclesiastical revenues, and that they would neither accept state pensions nor "government gifts."[20] When disestablishment was accomplished, however, they sought government grants for education, with a view to strengthening denominationalism in education. Meanwhile, the Irish Church Act and Fawcett's Act for the abolition of tests were bringing about changes in the direction of secularization at Trinity College. The passage of Fawcett's Act left the Divinity School completely in the hands of the Board of the College. Before disestablishment and the passing of Fawcett's Act, the Governing Body of the Divinity School was composed of members of the Irish Church, most of whom were in Holy Orders, and who, after disestablishment, could still wield their influence to maintain the Protestant character of Trinity College. Hence, after disestablishment, both Catholics and Protestants were still in a position to promote denominational education.

The Church Quarterly Review commented on secularization aspects of the change wrought at Trinity College as a result of disestablishment and of Fawcett's Act:

> All...is now changed. There is no security that the members of the Board in future will be members of the Church of Ireland, or even favourably disposed to her interests. The College is now being rapidly secularized by the diminution of the number of clerical Fellows and the subordinate

---

[20]Moran, op.cit., III, p. 71, "Letter to the Clergy and Laity of the Diocese Transmitting the Resolutions Adopted by the Irish Episcopate," October 9, 1867.

> place which is assigned in the college
> routine to theological instruction and to
> the chapel services.[21]

Gradually, there was no longer the obligation to attend catechetical lectures, and students were not required to go to chapel except on Sundays. Soon, undergraduates followed the example of some resident Fellows who neglected chapel attendance on weekdays. It is not surprising, therefore, that the disestablished Church expressed dissatisfaction with the Divinity School being controlled by a Board of such secularizing leanings.

Soon after disestablishment, the development of the secularizing trend at Trinity College, was reflected in the writings of many Protestant scholars to a marked degree. In 1871, Max Cullinan, Senior Moderator at Trinity College, made the following observation:

> The first proposition to be laid down with regard to Trinity College is, that the Divinity School must be totally disconnected from the College. This is a natural and necessary corollary to the Irish Church Bill. A regius professorship of divinity for a disestablished Church cannot be maintained...Probably the vested interests in the present Divinity School should be treated in the same way in which Maynooth has been treated.[22]

The reference to Maynooth was significant, and this plea for the secularization of Trinity College was intended to apply to the Catholic situation as well. Cullinan continued:

> As Trinity College should be rendered entirely non-denominational, so no system of denominational university education should be countenanced...The people and the Parliament which have signalized the nineteenth century, by putting an end to

---

[21]"Irish University Education and the Reform of Trinity College," Church Quarterly Review, Vol. LXIII (Oct. 1906 - Jan. 1907), p. 171.

[22]Max Cullinan, Trinity College, Dublin, and University Education in Ireland (London: Chapman and Hall, 1871), p. 73.

>an unrighteous Establishment, cannot now
>retrograde to the principles, practice and
>policy of the Middle Ages.[23]

Disestablishment, then, was at the center of the struggle between old and new ideas in Ireland. It represented the conflict between Irish Catholicism and British Liberalism. It sought an equilibrium between them, and finally a middle of the road solution of the university problem in Ireland. The Catholics, who were the immense majority in Ireland, wanted a Catholic University. Perhaps this was not unreasonable.

Elsewhere at that time, both Catholics and Protestants had universities where their sons were taught by persons of their own faith. Catholic France allowed the Protestants of Alsace to have the Protestant University of Strasbourg, Protestant Prussia allowed the Catholics of the Rhine to have the Catholic University of Bonn, the Protestants of Ireland were enjoying the privileges of Trinity College, or Dublin University, where the teachers and scholars were Protestants in Scotland there were similar universities, and at Oxford and Cambridge, England, most of the teachers were Anglicans.

As the Irish Catholics continued to seek redress in higher education, they were told that the Queen's Colleges were established specifically to meet their needs. But they did not want colleges created expressly for Ireland, instead, they sought colleges such as those in England and Scotland, but not after the pattern of the University of London. During the nineteenth century most students in Europe seemed to prefer universities of the type of Strasbourg, Bonn, and Oxford to that of the London model which was merely an examining body, and naturally, the Irish Catholics were of the same mind.

The Irish Catholics sustained well their claim to educational equality, but the clash of liberalism and Catholicism jeopardized the whole situation. There were those who felt that the Catholics had already gained as a result of disestablishment. In 1899, Anthony Trail repeated an earlier charge that Maynooth was provided for at the expense of Trinity College, in an article addressed to those who continued to press for a separately endowed Catholic University:

---

[23]<u>Ibid.</u>

> These persons seem altogether to have
> forgotten that the Roman Catholic Church
> has already been supplied with a divinity
> school and theological college richly endowed
> out of the confiscated funds of the Church of
> Ireland, and that this endowment is, out of all
> proportion, greater than the money expended
> upon the divinity school of Trinity College
> and more nearly proportioned to the whole
> endowments of Trinity College itself.[24]

On the other hand there were those who felt that Trinity College was left too well endowed after disestablishment. The Reverend Dr. John Healy, defending the Catholic position in 1890, wrote:

> Mr. Gladstone...succeeded in Disestablishing
> the Protestant Church; and it was hoped that
> he would also disestablish Trinity College, and
> either level up or down in the matter of endow-
> ment by dividing its revenues with the Catholic
> College, or endowing the latter on an equally
> liberal scale. It is hardly necessary for us
> to explain how these sanguine hopes were
> disappointed.[25]

Healy went on to show that the failure of the Irish University Bill of 1873 reflected some inconsistency between its principles and the hopes raised by the Irish Church Act. He charged that the language in which the Prime Minister at first announced his disestablishment policy, "was eminently calculated to foster this hope."[26]

Catholic higher education demands and expectations continued to receive attention from scholars and critics. In 1899, George Salmon made an observation on the Catholic demands, stating that what they had asked for was "a complete reversal of the principles on which English

---

[24] Anthony Trail, "Hands of Trinity," Nineteenth Century, XLV, March, 1899, p. 515.

[25] John Healy, "University Education in Ireland," Dublin Review, Vol. XXIII, January, 1890, p. 13.

[26] Ibid.

statesmen were agreed in 1869."[27] Salmon accused the Catholics for giving support to Mr. Gladstone on disestablishment which proclaimed the principle of State neutrality on religious questions "because they intended to make the doctrine of religious equality only a step towards placing their own Church in the position of pre-eminence from which the reformed Church was then deposed."[28] Very strongly Salmon declared that this has certainly proved to be the case as far as university education is concerned."[29] The Catholics were requesting a State-endowed university, which, though open to all, would be able to guard closely its highest prizes and its government for the benefit of their own Church. "This," Salmon wrote, "was exactly the position which Trinity College held before the disestablishment of the Irish Church, but which Parliament in 1873 pronounced improper to be occupied by the adherents of any one creed."[30]

It would be a mistake to conclude that the Irish Establishment did absolutely nothing to help people of other religious faiths. More than half a century before the Test Act of 1854 which admitted Nonconformists to membership at English universities, the degrees of Dublin University were thrown open to the world. This was the first university to grant degrees to Jews. In 1854, scholarships were created at Trinity College for students of any religious creed who objected to taking the declaration normally required of all candidates for certain foundation scholarships. In 1858, studentships, open to members of any religious faith, were established, and five out of the eighteen awards during the first nine years were given to Roman Catholics.

Not withstanding their disappointment with university reform in the aftermath of disestablishment, the Irish Catholic bishops could still reflect on the good that Trinity College represented in their midst. Her degrees in surgery were the earliest to be instituted or conferred, and her degrees in engineering were among the first to be offered in the British Isles. Certainly, these were benefits which both Protestants and Catholics shared in Ireland before disestablishment, and even after. Furthermore, F. Hugh O'Donnel raised an important

---

[27] George Salmon, "The Irish University Question," The Contemporary Review, Vol. LXXV, 1899. p. 596.

[28] Ibid.

[29] Ibid.

[30] Ibid.

issue when he insisted that the blame for what went wrong with Irish education rested with a combination of historical curcumstances, and not on the Establishment alone. Among other things, he considered that the failure of the Queen's Colleges was not due to the deonominational causes often alleged. The greatest undermining obstacles to progress were the absence of proper secondary education and "the clerical boycott of lay learning."[31]

Catholic laymen were ignored by their own clericals, by the Protestants, and by the Government. Of course, the Catholics said that it was nothing but the conscientious objections of the nation to the mixed education upheld by the Establishment which was causing the trouble. However, F. Hugh O'Donnell felt that "conscientious objection only existed for episcopal proclamations, and parliamentary consumption."[32] O'Donnell was most concerned about the art student of the Queen's College for there was no market for his brains. He was also concerned that "the schools and colleges which should be the natural resource of hundreds of gifted men, were shut against him."[33]

Another important point stressed by O'Donnell bore on the question of endowment of a Catholic university. The Catholic hierarchy before, and especially after disestablishment, made strong claims to State endowment of a Catholic institution. O'Donnell pointed out, however, that the real trouble lay with the Catholics themselves who misdirected huge sums of money at their disposal. He showed that out of the nearly ₤400,000 which Maynooth College received from the State after the Irish Church Act, less than ₤1,000 had been devoted to university requirements of the laity in Ireland. Of the ₤250,000 raised by the laity up to 1880, not a great deal was spent on university education.

According to O'Donnell, approximately ₤200,000 had been spent in the erection of costly and imposing Catholic churches and episcopal villas, "not one penny of which was allowed to be diverted to the missing requisites of Catholic University education."[34] O'Donnell

---

[31] F. Hugh O'Donnell, *The Ruin of Irish Education* (London: David Nutt, 1902), p. 24.

[32] Ibid., p. 28.

[33] Ibid., p. 26.

[34] Ibid., p. 12.

was himself a Catholic who seemed confounded at the neglect
of higher education finance by the hierarchy. While huge sums were spent
on clerical comforts, penury, misery, and dilapidation continued to be
the lot of the wretched edifices which still housed what was said to
be the burning aspiration and crying need of the Catholic intelligence
in Ireland.

The need for higher education reform prompted not only renewed
Catholic interest in disestablishment and disendowment, but also the hope
that State funds therefrom would be used for the endowment of a Catholic University. The Catholic laity, disappointed over the misuse of
the funds they collected for Catholic higher education during the first
years which still felt the impulsion of Dr. Newman's ideal, withdrew
support and henceforth gave money for everything else except a Catholic
University. It is true that when disestablishment came, they again rallied
behind the hierarchy, for then they perceived that some of the
resultant benefits would be in their favor.

At the time of disestablishment, the First Vatican Council
(1869-1870) issued a special invitation to the lay apostolate to
collaborate with the hierarchy for the express purpose of eliminating
errors and spreading the light of Christian faith. Before that time
the laity complained not only of the lack of cooperation on the part
of the hierarchy, but also of the exclusiveness of Maynooth College as a
place strictly for clerical learning. However, when disestablishment became a
reality, the Catholic bishops tended to relax their earlier stand against
lay education at Maynooth College.

Lack of provision for lay education at Maynooth College represented
one of the challenges to disestablishment. Gladstone's response
to the suggestion from Dr. C. W. Russell that Maynooth be considered
as an educational rather than an ecclesiastical establishment was
a threat to the entirely clerical nature of the college. The Catholic
leaders admitted, that, according to Gladstone, the State could then
intervene to regulate it, abolish tests or simply open it up to
laymen. They saw the danger in this, and consequently gave ground a
little. They agreed that if the College could not be dealt with
educationally without danger to its purposes, then it must form part
of a general settlement.

The bishops willingness to take part in a general arrangement was important to Maynooth's future, inasmuch as the
claim for purely educational consideration in the Church Act was

dropped. In 1876, Maynooth College became a College of the Catholic University, a result of the struggle for both lay and clerical education of Catholics. In 1882, the Catholic University of Ireland underwent a modification in its constitutions; this occurred, as Archbishop W. J. Walsh said, "in consequence of the necessity of working on the lines of the system of examinations that was practically forced upon the leading Catholic Colleges of Ireland by the establishment of the Royal University."[35]

The Royal University of 1879 was an interim settlement of the Irish university question which had been long pursued. That question had a very long and intricate history. Cardinal Cullen expressed hope in 1872 that Gladstone would bring peace to Ireland through a satisfactory university settlement, just as he had disestablished the Irish Church:

> May we not also expect that Mr. Gladstone and such Ministers as act with him will be anxious to fulfill the promises which they made years ago, and will endeavour, by introducing a satisfactory educational system for Ireland, to complete the work of pacification which they commenced by disestablishing the Irish Church and carrying the Land Act - two measures of great importance, well calculated to promote the public welfare of the country.[36]

Surely, the factor of education was just as important as matters in church and land in promoting the welfare of Ireland. Times were changing, and enlightened ideas had led men to concur that honor, wealth, power, and position should not be just the monopoly of the privileged classes. This was what disestablishment and the Irish Land Act signified. Greater changes could be wrought by education.

In his opening address at the first public meeting of the Royal University of Ireland, the Duke of Albercorn, Chancellor, emphasized the importance of education to the Irish people:

---

[35] W. J. Walsh, *The Irish University Question, The Catholic Case* (Dublin: Browne and Nolan Limited, 1897), p. 46.

[36] P. F. Moran, op.cit., III, p. 424, "Discourse on Catholic Education," delivered at a Meeting of the Catholics of Dublin, January 17, 1872, by Cardinal Cullen.

> By the great institution we are inaugurating today a still wider field is opened to them, which they may compete without let or hindrance or disadvantage, with the whole body of their fellow countrymen in every branch of literature and science, and with all the substantial rewards open to them that crown success.[37]

But while many leading Catholics agreed that the Royal University was a step in the right direction, they did not rest content. Archbishop Walsh viewed the continued predominance of Trinity College as a grave and irritating drawback, which could not be eliminated by any liberality in the mere matter of endowment. Walsh, like many other Catholics, was still worried about inequality and concluded that as regards University privileges, and University status in Ireland, "no Catholic college can hold a position other than one of tangible and humiliating inferiority, in contrast with the position of Trinity College."[38]

The submission of Archbishop Walsh that the formidable position of Trinity College was likely to prolong inequality of educational opportunity, was tantamount to a recognition of the limited extent of the implications of disestablishment for Catholic objectives in higher education in Ireland. Religious equality was the principal issue as well as the main consequence of disestablishment; educational equality was but an offshoot.

---

[37] First Report of the Royal University of Ireland, Dublin, 1883, Appendix I, p. 10.

[38] W. J. Walsh, op.cit., p. 45.

BIBLIOGRAPHY

A. OFFICIAL PAPERS

Great Britain.   Hansard's Parliamentary Debates (Third Series)
                 Vols. LXXXI (1845), CLXXI (1863), CLXXVIII -
                 CLXXXII (1865), CLXXXVII (1867), and CXC -
                 CCXIV (1868-1873).

Great Britain.   Parliamentary Papers.
                 Annual Report of the Commissioners of Education
                 in Ireland to His Excellency the Lord Lieutenant
                 for the Year 1854-55, 1854-55, XVI, 23.

                 Commission for Inquiring Into the Management and
                 Government of the College of Maynooth, 1855, XXII, 1.

                 Endowed Schools Ireland Commission, 1858, XXII,
                 Part I.

                 The Twenty-sixth Report of the Commissioners of
                 National Education in Ireland (for the Year 1859),
                 1860, XXVI, Part I.

                 Copies of the Petitions of the Provost, Fellows, and
                 Scholars of Trinity College, Dublin, under Corporate
                 Seal dated the 12th day of June, 1868, 1870, LIV, 637.

                 Report of a Visitation held at Maynooth College on
                 the 20th day of June, 1860, 1860, LIII, 649.

                 Copies of a Memorial addressed by the Trustees of
                 the Royal College of St. Patrick, Maynooth, to the
                 Lord Lieutenant of Ireland, with respect to the
                 Repairs of the College, 1860, LIII, 655.

                 Report of the Visitors of Maynooth, 1864, 1865,
                 XLIII, 451.

                 Correspondence between Her Majesty's Government and
                 the Commissioners of National Education (Ireland) on
                 the Subject of the Organization and Government of
                 Training and Model Schools, 1866, LV, 213.

Copies of Memorials addressed to the Secretary of State for the Home Department by Roman Catholic prelates in Ireland on the Subject of National and University Education in Ireland, and of the Correspondence relating thereto, 1866, LV, 243.

Report of the Oaths Commission, 1867, XXXI, 40.

Correspondence Relative to the Proposed Charter to a Roman Catholic University in Ireland, 1867-68, LIII, 779.

A Bill to put an end to the Establishment of the Irish Church, and to make Provision in respect of the Temporalities thereof, and in respect of the Royal College of Maynooth, 1868-69, III, 85.

A Bill to amend the Law relating to the Occupation of Land in Ireland, 1870, II, 259.

A Bill to Amend the Act of the First and Second Years of His Late Majesty, King William the Fourth, chapter thirty-three in part, and to afford facilities for the erection, enlargement and improvement of Glebe Houses and for the acquirements of Lands and Glebes in Ireland, 1870, II, 169.

Declaration of the Catholic Laity of Ireland on the Subject of University Education in that country, 1870, LIV, 645.

Commission of Inquiry into Primary Education (Ireland), 1870, XVII, 1.

Copy of Declaration of Heads of Roman Catholic Colleges and Schools and Other Persons lately laid before the Prime Minister, 1870, LIV, 601.

Petition of Certain Graduates of the University of Trinity College, Dublin, presented on March 6, 1868, to the Honourable, the House of Commons of the United Kingdom of Great Britain and Ireland in Parliament assembled, 1870, LIV, 637.

Copies of the Petitions of the Provost, Fellows and Scholars of Trinity College, Dublin, under Corporate Seal, dated the 12th day of June, 1868, 1870, LIV, 637.

University Test Act, 1871, VI, 535.

A Bill to provide facilities for the purchase of
Lands by Tenants in Ireland and Amend and Alter
Part II and Part III of the Landlord and Tenant
(Ireland) Act 1870, 1873, II, 285.

Irish University Bill 1873, 1873, VI, 329.

Resolutions of the Standing Committee (on Trinity
College) of the General Assembly of the Irish
Presbyterian Church on the Subject of the Irish
University Bill, 1873, LII, 491.

Return of the Total Revenue from All Sources of
Trinity College, Dublin, for each Year from 1869
to 1873, 1874, LI, 701.

Copy of Declaration of Catholic Laity in Ireland
on the Subject of University Education in that
Country, 1878-79, LVII, 495.

A Bill to Make Better Provision for University
Education in Ireland, 1879, VII, 577.

Report of the Intermediate Education Board for
the Year 1879, 1880, XXIII, 31.

Report of the Commissioners of Church Temporalities
in Ireland for the period 1869-1880, 1881, XXVIII, 61.

A Bill to afford Increased Facilities for obtaining
Sites for Places of Worship Schools, and Residences
for teachers and clergymen in Ireland, 1883, IX, 259.

Trinity College, Dublin; Return showing the Cross
and Nett Revenues for the Year 1888, 1889, LIX, 389.

Trinity College, Dublin, Estates Commission, 1904,
1905, XXVII, 81.

B. COLLECTIONS OF LETTERS, DIARIES AND SPEECHES

Bassett, A. Tilney (ed.), Gladstone's Speeches, London: Methuen and Co. Ltd., 1916.

_____, Gladstone to His Wife, London: Methuen and Co. Ltd., 1936.

Buckle, George Earle (ed.), The Letters of Queen Victoria, 1862-1885, Second Series, 3 Vols., London: John Murray, 1928.

Daunt, W. J. O'Neill, A Life Spent for Ireland, being selections from the Journals of the late W. J. O'Neill Daunt edited by his daughter, London: T. Fisher Unwin, 1896.

DeVere, Aubrey, Recollections of Aubrey deVere, New York: E. Arnold, 1897.

Gladstone, William Ewart, A Chapter of Autobiography, London: John Murray, 1868.

_____, A Correct Report of the Speech of the Right Hon. W. E. Gladstone on Proposing the Irish Land Bill, February 15, 1870, London: John Murray, 1870.

_____, The Gladstone Papers, London: Cassell and Co. Ltd., 1930.

_____, Speeches of the Right Hon. W. E. Gladstone, M.P., delivered at Warrington, Ormskirk, Liverpool, Southport, Newton, Leigh and Wigan in October, 1868, London: Simpkin, Marshall and Company, 1868.

_____, Speeches of the Right Honourable William Ewart Gladstone, M.P., in Southwest Lancashire, October, 1868, Liverpool: Egerton Smith and Co., 1868.

_____, The Irish Church. A Speech delivered in the House of Commons on Monday, March 1, 1869, London: John Murray, 1869.

Guedalla, Philip (ed.), The Queen and Mr. Gladstone, 1845-1879, 2 vols., London: Hodder and Stoughton, Ltd., 1933.

Kimberley, John, First Earl of, A Journal of Events During the Gladstone Ministry, 1868-1874, London: Offices of the Royal Historical Society, 1958.

Lathbury, D. C. (ed.), Correspondence on Church and Religion of William Ewart Gladstone, 2 vols., London: John Murray, 1910.

Lucy, Henry W., A Diary of Two Parliaments, 2 vols., London: Cassell and Company Limited, 1885.

Moran, Patrick, Francis (ed.), The Pastoral Letters and Other Writings of Cardinal Cullen, 3 vols., Dublin: Browne and Nolan, 1882.

Ramm, Agatha (ed.), The Political Correspondence of Mr. Gladstone and Lord Granville, 1868-1876, 2 vols., London: Offices of the Royal Historical Society, 1952.

Shane, Leslie, "Irish Pages from the Postbags of Manning, Cullen and Gladstone," in Dublin Review, October, 1919.

C. CONTEMPORARY PERIODICALS AND NEWSPAPERS

Annual Register (London)

Blackwood's Magazine (Edinburgh)

Contemporary Review (London)

Church Quarterly Review (London)

Catholic University Bulletin (Washington, D.C.)

Dublin Review (London)

Edinburgh Review (Edinburgh)

Freeman's Journal (Dublin)

Weekly Freeman's Journal (Dublin)

Irish Ecclesiastical Record (Dublin)

The Month (London)

Quarterly Review (London)

Saturday Review (London)

Nation (New York)

Nineteenth Century (London)

Fortnightly Review (London)

The Times (London)

D. PAMPHLETS AND WORKS BY CONTEMPORARIES

Brady, W. Maziere, Some Remarks on the Irish Church Bill, London: Longmans, Green and Co., 1869.

Butt, Isaac, The Problem of Irish Education, London: Longmans, Green and Co., 1875.

Calvert, Frederick, Denominationalists and Secularists, London: W. Ridgway, 1876.

Cullinan, Max, Trinity College, Dublin, and University Education in Ireland, London: Chapman and Hall, 1871,

Dixon, W. MacNeille, Trinity College, Dublin, London: F. E. Robinson and Co., 1902.

Healy, John, Maynooth College, Its Centenary History, 1795-1895, Dublin, 1895.

Ireland, Board of National Education, Report of the Board of National Education in Ireland for the Year 1875, Dublin: Alexander Thom, 1876.

Lawless, Emily, Ireland, London: T. Fisher Unwin, (1887).

McCarthy, Justin, A History of Our Own Times, 4 vols., London: Chatto and Windus, 1880.

Maguire, Thomas, The Maynooth Resolutions Considered, Dublin: William McGee, 1869.

Molesworth, William, History of England from 1830-1874, Abridged
          edition, London: Chapman and Hall, Limited, 1889.

O'Donnell, F. Hugh, The Ruin of Irish Education, London: David Nutt,
          1902.

Pim, Jonathan, The Irish University Question, London: Hodges, Fostor
          and Co., 1874.

Pope, Thomas, The Council of the Vatican and the Events of the Times,
          Boston: Patrick Donahoe, 1872.

Royal University, First Report of the Royal University of Ireland,
          Dublin: Alex, Thom and Co., 1883.

Walsh, W. J. The Irish University Question: The Catholic Case,
          Dublin: Browne and Nolan, 1897.

E. BIOGRAPHIES

MacSuibhne, Peadar, Paul Cullen and His Contemporaries, 1820-1902,
          Kildare: Leinster Leader Ltd., 1965, Vol. III.

Magnus, Philip, Gladstone: A Biography, London: John Murray, 1954.

Monypenny, W. F. and Buckle, G. E., The Life of Benjamin Disraeli,
          Rev. ed., 2 vols., New York: The Macmillan Co., 1929.

Morley, John, The Life of William Ewart Gladstone, New edition, 3 vols.,
          New York: The MacMillan Co., 1911.

Purcell, Edmund S., Life of Cardinal Manning, 2 vols., New York:
          Macmillan and Company, 1895.

Trevelyan, G. M., The Life of John Bright, London: Constable and
          Company Limited, 1913.

Index

Archbishop Cullen, 5
  Criticism of Board of Education, 7
  On educational equality, 8,11
  On Anglican Church property, 20
  Opposition to mixed education, 37
  Hostility to Queen's Colleges, 65,90
  Condemnation of the Irish University Bill of 1873, 89
Archbishop Leahy of Cashel, 23,54
Archbishop Manning, 2,6,10,93

Blackwood's Magazine, 70,82
Bright, John 3,5,53
Brotherhood Fenian, 9,10,11
Bruce, H.H., 13,53
Bryce, James, 103
Butt, Isaac, 58,97,98,99

Catholic hierarchy, 1,2,6,7,62
Catholic laity, 38,39
Catholic University, 66,105
Chadwick, W.O., 78

Chapter of Autobiography, 28
Christian Brothers, 67
Church Quarterly Review, 115
Church question, 18,19,20,21,23,83,98
Church-State relationship, 20
College, Maynooth, (See Maynooth College); Trinity (See Trinity College)
Colleges, Queen's, 78,100,101
Commission, Powis, 35,36; Robertson, 102
Concurrent endowment, 6
Coinper Temple Clause, 77
Council, First Vatican, 123
Cullen, Archbishop (See Archbishop Cullen)

- 133 -

de Vere, Aubrey, 22
Denominational education, 77,96
Deary, John, 23
Disendowment, 2,50
Disestablishment, 27,33,50,70,71,81,96,118
Disraeli, Benjamin, 25
Dissenters, English, 9,82
Don,T. O'Connor, 27,28
Dorrian, Bishop Patrick, 14
Dublin Review, 5,18,27,82,105
Duffy Patrick, 49

Edinburgh Review, 76
Education, intermediate, 69; denominational, 77,96; united secular, 78,82
Educational equality, 7,8,36,48,71
Endowment, 19
English Dissenters, 9,82
English Liberation Society, 2
Equality, educational, (See educational equality)
Equality, religious, 36

Fawcett, Henry, 33,113
Fenian Brotherhood, 9,10,11
Fenianism, 10
First Vatican Council, 123
Fortescue, Chichester, 25
Free Royal Schools, 68
Freeman's Journal, The Weekly, 4

Gagging clauses, 92
Gladstone, W.E., 3
  On the university question, 9
  Impact of Fenian explosion at Clerkenwell prison, 1867, 9,10
  Concern for Ireland, 12
  Divided attitude toward Ireland, 13
  Determination to settle difficult Irish problems, 14
  Sought to end Establishment in 1868, 20,21
  Favored secularization, 22

   Higher education and church problems interwined, 22
   Opposition to policy of concurrent endowment, 22,29
   Election promises, 27
   Favored governing Ireland along Irish lines, 31,32
   On significance of abortive Irish University Bill of 1873, 94
Glebe Loans Bill, 54
Glebes question, 53
Gray, Sir John, 5
Grey, Sir George, 8

Hamilton, Lord Claud, 14
Hanly, Esq., James, 30
Hierarchy, Catholic, (See Catholic Hierarchy)
Home Rule, 39

Intermediate education, 69
Intermediate Education Board, 71
Irish Anglican Church Establishment, 19,31,70,94

Irish Church Act of 1869, 28,101
<u>Irish Ecclesiastical Record</u>, 73
Irish University Act of 1879, 95
Irish University Bill of 1873, 88,89,95
Irish University Bill of 1879, 95
Irish Revolutionary Brotherhood, (See Fenian Brotherhood)

Kavanagh, James, 31
Keane, William, 52

Land Act of 1870, 57,59,122
Land question, 4,41,43,49,50,53,57,62,63
Laws, penal, 20
Leahy, Patrick (See Archbishop Leahy of Cashel)

MacSweeney, Peter Paul, 52,56
Maguire, J.F., 11,72,73
Manning, Archbishop, (See Archbishop Manning)
Maynooth College, 20,24,25,44,45,46,81
Maynooth Resolutions, 4,31,36,42 Mayo, Lord, 1,8
Mixed education, 14,35,72,97
Monsell, William, 81
Moriarty, David, 9,11, <u>Month The</u>, 104
Morris, William O'Connor, 69

National Association, The, 2,21
National University of Ireland, 104
Newdgate, C.N., 11
Nonconformists, (See English Dissenters)

O'Donnell F. Hugh, 121
O'Donoghue, T, 65
O'Hea, Michael, 52
Oath taking, 24

Penal laws, 20
Plunkett, William, 65, Pope, Thomas, 29
Powis Commission, 35,36, Presbyterians, 91
Proselytism, 18,30
Protestant ascendancy, 3,44,61,70,71

Quarterly Review, 110
Queen's Colleges, 79,100,101
Queen's University, 100

Religious equality, 36
Robertson Commission, 102
Royal University of 1880, 97,99,100
Russell, C.W., 11,13,80

Salmon, George, 119
Saturday Review, 37,42,50,59,76
Secularization, 21,116,117

Temporalities Act of 1833, 108 Tenants Purchase Act of 1873, 62
Thompson, William, 37
Times, The, 13,37,49
Trinity College, 8,18,19,42,43,44,46,73

Ulster Tenant Right, 51,112
Ultramontanism, 11,81
University education question, 6,10,67,70,73,81,83,85
United secular education, 74,82
Upas Tree, 1,50,70
Universities Test Act of 1871, 77

Voluntaryism, 7,8

Whitesdie, James, 114
Wodehouse, Lord, 7,13
Wyse, Thomas, 55

Young Islandism, 9

- 136 -